John Lucas is the author of five books, including *Hertfordshire Curiosities* (also published by the Dovecote Press), and a descriptive guide to London's 100 museums. He was born in Winchmore Hill, North London, and traces his family back to 1750 in Hertfordshire. He now lives in Potters Bar. He began in journalism as a reporter on the *Barnet Press*, becoming a founder member of the *Sunday Telegraph*, and more recently chief sub-editor and feature writer with *Daily Telegraph Weekend*.

Following page
Pitstone Windmill.

Buckinghamshire Curiosities

John Lucas

THE DOVECOTE PRESS

*To the memory of Lt Clyde ('Sparky') Cosper, US Air Force,
who gallantly sacrificed his life to save
the town of Princes Risborough*

First published in 1993 by the Dovecote Press Ltd
Stanbridge, Wimborne, Dorset BH21 4JD

ISBN 1 874336 11 3

© John Lucas 1993
Phototypeset in Times by The Typesetting Bureau
6 Church St, Wimborne, Dorset
Printed and bound in Singapore

Contents

Introduction

Buckinghamshire is among the most fortunate of counties. At its nearest point it is only eighteen miles from London, yet it remains at a safe enough distance to enjoy rural peace. This book is about another aspect of Buckinghamshire's personality: its 'curious' side. 'Curiosity' is a flexible enough word to embrace what is surprising, interesting, unusual or strange, or perhaps something of each. But what is 'curious' to one person may not be to another, so the author of a book such as this makes a judgment that is largely subjective; he hopes what interests him will also interest his readers.

In these pages, rather than merely identifying monuments, buildings or people, I have sought to set them in their historical context - whether it is John Hampden's statue in Aylesbury, the martyrs' memorial on the hillside above Amersham, or the 'Enigma' building in Bletchley Park.

Two cautionary points. It is a sad sign of the times that, because of vandalism, many churches find it necessary to remain closed for much of the week. The best opportunity of visiting them is, of course, around the time of Sunday services. It should also be noted that all National Trust properties (marked NT in text) except Cliveden close on two days a week. These days vary from property to property, and visitors should play safe by telephoning first to check opening times.

No book of this kind can be compiled without the help of many people, of whom the following deserve particular mention, with my thanks: Ian Horwood, of Stokenchurch, for information about the custom of weighing in the Mayor of High Wycombe and for permission to reproduce a photograph; the regional office of the National Trust at Hughenden Manor; Rosemary Jury, of the National Trust at Stowe; Jocelyne Reddington; D. E. R. Revel and M. J. Ambrose, of Wycombe Cemetery; Roy Spicer; Frances Watt; Richard Wells, Editor of *The Bucks Herald,* and members of his team, for information and the photograph of the Cosper memorial at Princes Risborough ; Carol Wright, for her sketches; Aylesbury Tourist Information Office; and the ever-willing staff of Buckinghamshire County Library.

Finally, I hope you enjoy your excursions into Buckinghamshire as much as I have done.

John Lucas

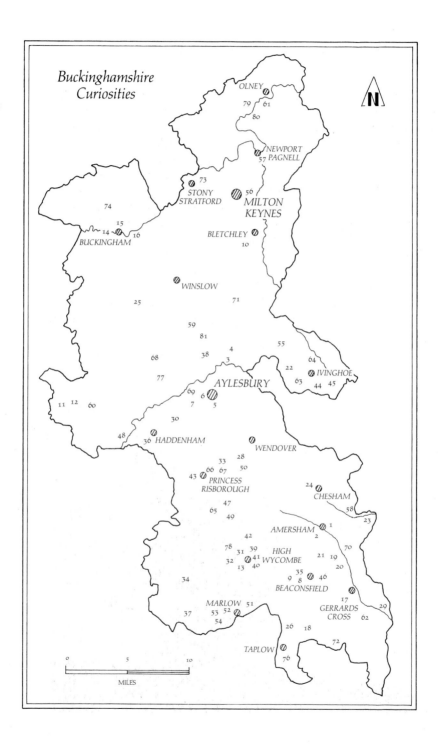

Buckinghamshire
Curiosities

N

OLNEY
79 61
80

NEWPORT
PAGNELL
57

73
STONY
STRATFORD

56
MILTON
KEYNES

74

15
14   16
BUCKINGHAM

BLETCHLEY
10

WINSLOW

25   71

59
81

68   38   4   55
3   64
77   22   IVINGHOE
AYLESBURY   63   44 45
69 6
7 5

11 12 60

30

48
36 HADDENHAM   WENDOVER

33 28
66 67 50
43   24 CHESHAM
PRINCESS
RISBOROUGH   58
47   23
65   49

42   AMERSHAM 1
78 31 39   2
32   41 HIGH   70
13 40 WYCOMBE   21 19
35   20
34   9 8 46
BEACONSFIELD
17
GERRARDS 29
MARLOW 51   CROSS 62
37 53 52
54   26 18
72
TAPLOW 76

0   5   10

MILES

1 When Life was a Grind

The winds that sweep across Aylesbury Vale and over the Chiltern Hills once fed windmills. Although the sails may not turn today, half a dozen have survived to be lovingly restored, and are open to view, making glorious decorative features on the Buckinghamshire skyline.

Pitstone Mill, a few hundred yards south of *Ivinghoe* (map ref: SP 945/156), has a fair claim to being the oldest in Britain, for one timber bears the date 1627. This post mill – the earliest form of mill – was badly damaged in a freak storm in 1902, and could no longer operate. It was given to the National Trust in 1937 by a local farmer, L. J. Hawkins, of the nearby Pitstone Green Farm, and after 1963 was restored by volunteers. It is open to the public May to September on Sundays and Bank Holidays (Tel: 0582 600391).

Bradwell Tower Mill, *New Bradwell*, Milton Keynes (map ref: SP 831/411), was built in about 1816, of local limestone, and was in use until 1871. Its cap has an upturned boat shape and a raised walkway for tending the sails. Under restoration.

Brill Windmill, about 10 miles west of *Aylesbury* (map ref: SP

Brill Windmill.

652/142), is a weatherboarded post mill with a brick protected base. It dates from 1668 and was used until 1916. Can be visited on Sunday afternoons (Tel: 0844 237060).

Lacey Green Windmill, Windmill Farm, *Lacey Green,* near Aylesbury (map ref: SP 819/009), is thought to be the oldest surviving smock mill in England. Originally erected at Chesham in 1650, it was moved to its present site in 1821. It is being restored by the Chiltern Society. Open May to September, Suns only (Tel: 08444 3560.)

Quainton Windmill, north-west of *Aylesbury* (map ref: SP 746/203) is a tower mill built circa 1830 with bricks made on the site; it is 65 ft high and has six floors. It is now being restored to working order (Tel: 0296 75348 or 75440).

The 12-sided smock mill, Cobstone Mill, at *Turville*, a village about five miles south-west of High Wycombe (map ref: SU 770/915), has been converted into a private house. It can clearly be seen on Turville Hill overlooking the village. The mill was featured in the film 'Chitty Chitty Bang Bang'.

The hillside memorial to the Amersham Martyrs.

2 Martyrs' Memorial

Position: Amersham is 2 miles from Herts border to the east.
O.S. Map: Aylesbury area; Sheet 165; 1/50,000.
Map Ref: SU 963/977.
Access: Path from cemetery behind St Mary's Church in Market Square, to top of hill, then right. Or along path off Station Road signposted 'Martyrs' Memorial' (above Ruckles Way).

On a sunny summer's afternoon, no event could be further from the mind than the one commemorated by the granite obelisk here, erected by the Protestant Alliance in 1931. All but hidden on a hillside above Amersham, it is a sombre memorial to England's intolerant past. In 1506 and 1521, about 100 yards from the memorial, seven Protestants – six men and one woman – were burned at the stake.

'The Noble Army of Martyrs Praise Thee – Amersham Martyrs', reads the inscription. 'They died for the principles of religious liberty, for the right to read and interpret the Holy Scriptures and to worship God according to their consciences as revealed through God's Holy Word.'

At the burnings, the cruelty was compounded in one case by forcing children to light their father's pyre; in another, the task fell to a married daughter.

These martyrs were Lollards, active followers of the movement initiated by the 14th-century reformer John Wycliffe, translator of the Bible into English and a vigorous attacker of many alleged abuses in the established Church (of Rome).

In the Chilterns area there was a Lollard revival in around 1500, and while most sympathisers, under pressure from the bishops, 'abjured' (i.e. recanted their beliefs), others refused. These would be handed over to the civil power and burnt – as in the case of the Amersham martyrs.

Places of Interest in the Neighbourhood
An Unfaithful Queen (Chenies)
Puddingstone Church (Chesham)
Honour for a Horse (Latimer)

3 A Lost Village

Position: Aston Abbotts is 3 miles NE of Aylesbury.
O.S. Map: Aylesbury area; Sheet 165; 1/50,000.
Map Ref: SP 842/188.
Access: Outlines are visible along the gated road from Aston Abbotts to
Weedon.

Travelling from Aston Abbotts along the gated road towards Weedon
village, one can pause on Line's Hill, look down to the left and see the
remains of the ghost village of Burston to the south. They appear as
ridged outlines in a meadow where sheep are usually grazing.

One story is that in the early 16th century the lord of the manor told
the villagers that because he wanted to graze his sheep on the common
land they were using, they were to be evicted and their homes destroyed.
Another is that the villager was wiped out by disease, perhaps plague.

Places of Interest in the Neighbourhood
President's Bus Stop (Aston Abbotts)
Norman Glory (Stewkley)
Birthplace of Mrs Miniver (Whitchurch)

Aston Abbotts's bus shelter, the gift of President Benes.

4 President's Bus Stop

Position: Aston Abbotts is about 3 miles NE of Aylesbury.
O.S. Map: Aylesbury area; Sheet 165; 1/50,000.
Map Ref: SP 858/197.
Access: At crossroads with A418, half a mile SE of village.

The brick-built bus shelter at this crossroads looks perfectly ordinary, and no more notable than any other. In fact it has a special history, connected with the Second World War, when many foreign governments-in-exile were based in Britain.

In Aston Abbotts – at The Abbey, which overlooks the village green – lived President Eduard Benes of Czechoslovakia, whose Cabinet, which included Foreign Minister Jan Masaryk, stayed at Wingrave Manor.

A warm friendship grew up between the Czech exiles and the people of the two villages, and it was here that the Czech intelligence services planned how to free their country from the Nazi invaders. The assassination of the Nazi dictator of Czechoslovakia, 'Butcher' Heydrich, was worked out here.

After the war, the bus shelter was the personal parting gift to the people of Aston Abbotts from the President when he and his Government returned home in 1945. He had often seen people standing in chilly discomfort at the bus stop, so he left money for the shelter, and play equipment for the local school, now a restaurant. He also planted a lime tree, which still thrives, on the approach to The Abbey. President Benes led the Government in his homeland until the Communists seized power in 1948, the year he died.

A previous occupier of The Abbey was the English Polar explorer, Rear Admiral Sir James Clark Ross, whose tomb is in the churchyard. He lived at Aylesbury. The east windows in the church at Aston are in his memory. His great achievement was discovering the position of the North magnetic Pole (which varies by about six degrees west of true north) in 1831. He subsequently worked on the magnetic survey of Great Britain, and commanded the ships *Erebus* and *Terror* on the Antarctic expedition of 1839-1843, for which he was knighted.

Places of Interest in the Neighbourhood
A Lost Village (Aston Abbotts)
Norman Glory (Stewkley)
Birthplace of Mrs Miniver (Whitchurch)

5 When Hampden said 'No'

Position: Aylesbury is about 14 miles S of Milton Keynes.
O.S. Map: Aylesbury area; Sheet 165; 1/50,000.
Map Ref: SP 818/137.
Access: From A41 (T); Market Square is in the town centre.

The imposing bronze statue of the Buckinghamshire squire and land-owner John Hampden, by H. C. Fehr (1912), in Aylesbury's Market Square commemorates his refusal to pay Ship Money – a tax to support the navy – to Charles I – an act of defiance that secured him his place in history.

Hampden had harboured a grudge against the King for imprisoning him 10 years earlier for refusing to pay a 'forced loan' for his war in France. Later, Charles tried to extend to places inland the ship tax on coastal towns to support the navy in an emergency. He was entitled to levy the tax without Parliament's approval only in a national emergency, which Hampden claimed didn't exist.

In 1637, seven judges ruled against Hampden, and five for – so he had to pay. The narrow legal decision helped finally to undermine England's absolute monarchy and led to the Civil War. Hampden fought on the Parliamentary side, but in 1643 at Chalgrove Field (map ref: SU 644/977) he was fatally wounded and died six days later at the age of 49.

Hampden's family home was in Great Hampden (about six miles south of Aylesbury, map ref: SP 845/015). There is a monument in Prestwood, where the land on which he refused to pay the tax was situated (see 'In Memory of Hampden'). In the Church of St Nicholas at Great Kimble (map ref: SP 825/067), where he publicly announced his refusal to pay Ship Money, there is a facsimile of the document.

Places of Interest in the Neighbourhood
Cromwell Sat Here (Aylesbury)
Evergreen Response (Aylesbury)
Unknown Warriors (Hardwick)

John Hampden's statue in Aylesbury town centre.

6 Cromwell Sat Here

Position: Aylesbury is about 14 miles S of Milton Keynes.
O.S. Map: Aylesbury area; Sheet 165; 1/50,000.
Map Ref: SP 818/138.
Access: The King's Head is in George Street, off Market Square, in the town centre.

After his victory at the Battle of Worcester in 1651, Cromwell stayed at the King's Head in George Street, and the chair he reputedly sat in can be seen in that rarity, a public house owned by the National Trust.

The first mention of the 'Kyngeshede' was in 1455. In its early days the inn was the guest house of a monastery, later becoming a coaching inn. Passing through the medieval gateway and into the lounge, the visitor sees a fine pre-Tudor leaded window containing its original glass. Two panes from the windows in the room now form part of a window in Westminster Abbey, and three more are in the British Museum.

Places of Interest in the Neighbourhood
Evergreen Response (Aylesbury)
When Hampden said 'No' (Aylesbury)
Unknown Warriors (Hardwick)

Saying it with flowers, the memorial to Lady Lee.

7 Evergreen Response

Position: Aylesbury is about 14 miles S of Milton Keynes.
O.S. Map: Aylesbury area; Sheet 165; 1/50,000.
Map Ref: SP 817/139.
Access: St Mary's Church is reached up the path from Parson's Fee.

A request made more than 400 years ago is still being honoured in the 13th-century parish church of St Mary, in Aylesbury. One of the monuments, in the north transept, is to the wife and three children of Sir Henry Lee, personal Champion of Elizabeth I and an ancestor of Robert E. Lee, the general who led the southern armies in the American Civil War.

An inscription on the tomb of Lady Lee notes that she bore 'three impes', John, Henry and Mary. The first two died in youth and the third 'in flower, and in the prime of all her years'. The verse goes on:

'Goodfrend, sticke not to strew with crimson flowers
This marble stone wherin her cindres rest
For sure her ghost lives with the heavenly powers
And guerdon hathe of virtuous life possest?'

Faithful to this request, a member of the the congregation ensures that the tomb is never without its red flowers, which have been set there since Lady Lee's death in 1584. Her tomb was moved here from nearby Quarrendon, where she and Sir Henry lived in the manor (see No 69).

Places of Interest in the Neighbourhood
Cromwell Sat Here (Aylesbury)
When Hampden Said No (Aylesbury)
Unknown Warriors (Hardwick)

8 It's a Small World

Position: Beaconsfield is SE of High Wycombe.
O.S. Map: Reading & Windsor area; Sheet 175; 1/50,000.
Map Ref: SU 940/914.
Access: Turn off M40 (junction 2), then take the A355 to Beaconsfield.
Bekonscot is in Warwick Rd.

Bekonscot Model Village has been demonstrating for many years that small is beautiful. It was in 1929 that Roland Callingham and his friend, James Shilcock, opened it to the public, since when it has raised more than 3 million pounds for charity.

Bekonscot, occupying 4,400 square yards, is an idealised village of the 1930s, in an impressive setting of conifers, dwarf trees and shrubs, and evergreen ground-cover plants – a horticultural study in themselves.

It's some village. Designed to a scale of one inch to one foot, it has three castles, several churches (hymn-singing can be heard), pubs, several railway lines with trains speeding along between timbered houses, thatched cottages and shops, and stopping at the stations. A large white windmill dominates the scene, which contains a racecourse and a hunt in progress. As well as a fairground, there is a harbour with pier, bridge, ships and a lighthouse. The whole is an impressive example of the model-maker's art.

Throughout its life, Bekonscot has had a strong connection with the Church Army, which in 1978 set up a special company to administer it. The village is open from March to October, but closes in winter for painting, repairs and renovations. (Tel: 0494 672919.)

Places of Interest in the Neighbourhood
Rector v. Farmers (Beaconsfield)
A Standard of Loyalty (Forty Green)
Return of the Mayflower (Jordans)

The famous Bekonscot model village at Beaconsfield.

9 Rector v. Farmers

Position: Holtspur, just west of Beaconsfield.
O.S. Map: Reading, Windsor area; Sheet 175; 1/50,000.
Map Ref: SU 927/898.
Access: The Tithing Stone is on the north side of the A40 between North Drive and Burgess Wood Road.

The Tithing Stone commemorates a notable tussle between local farmers and the Rev John Gould, rector of St Mary and All Saints, Beaconsfield (about a mile eastwards, ref: SU 946/900), over the old system of levying the tithe. Farmers had to pay to the church a 'tax', or tithe, equalling one-tenth of the value of what they produced. But the farmers maintained that if the corn was collected after it had been stacked into shocks for drying, it was worth more because of the extra labour involved, and the proportion due should be reduced from one in every ten shocks to only one in every eleven.

The Tithing Stone, two feet or so high, was the boundary stone of the manor and parish of Beaconsfield. An inscription, dated 1827, notes that the 'custom of tithing corn in this Parish is (as has been so immemorially) by the tenth cock and the eleventh shock'. In other words, one-tenth before the corn dried, but only one-eleventh afterwards.

The Rev Gould, longest-serving rector of the church (46 years), ended his days in Newgate Prison for debt. He died in 1866.

Places of Interest in the Neighbourhood
It's a Small World (Beaconsfield)
A Standard of Loyalty (Forty Green)
Return of the *Mayflower* (Jordans)

The Tithing Stone memorial at Holtspur, Beaconsfield.

10 Solving the Enigma

Position: Bletchley Park is just NW of Bletchley BR station.
O.S. Map: Northampton, Milton Keynes; Sheet 152; 1/50,000.
Map Ref: SP 865/343.
Access: From Wilton Avenue, off Church Green Road.

Bletchley Park and its Victorian mansion have a distinguished recent history. At the outbreak of the Second World War the park's 55 acres formed the HQ of the Government's Code and Cipher School. Here, thousands of scientists, mathematicians and code experts were able to eavesdrop on many of Hitler's closely guarded secrets, hidden by his enciphering system, Enigma.

Decrypting these messages was at first a cooperative effort between the British and the French, using pre-war pioneer work by Polish mathematicians. In May 1940, three months before the London Blitz, the code-breakers were able to read every message sent out from German Air Force headquarters to commanders in the field.

Bletchley Park's work was code-named Ultra, and its code-breaking activities proved vital at Dunkirk, the victory of the desert armies in North Africa, the battle of the Atlantic and the Normandy invasion in 1944. In a letter of thanks in July 1945, General Eisenhower said the Park's work had been of priceless value to him in saving thousands of

The wartime house of secrets in Bletchley Park.

British and American lives.

After the war, the Park continued to be used by the intelligence services and other agencies, but was decommissioned in 1987. The house is a Grade I listed building; the park still contains many of the wartime buildings, and there are plans to convert these into a museums campus.

Places of Interest in the Neighbourhood
A City Clad in Green (Milton Keynes)
Allotted Span (Newport Pagnell)
Tall Stories (Stony Stratford)

The net funnel used to trap ducks at Boarstall Decoy.

11 Out for the Ducks

Position: Boarstall is about 11 miles W of Aylesbury.
O.S. Map: Aylesbury area; Sheet 165; 1/50,000.
Map Ref: SP 623/152.
Access: The Duck Decoy (NT) is off B4011, from A41 (T).

Boarstall Duck Decoy is a strange centuries-old survival from the days
when ducks intended for the table were lured into nets, set in chan-
nels leading off lakes. In the 19th century, they were considered a
cheap method of trapping wildfowl for the table, and a decoyman was
retained for the work.

   Boarstall's decoy, which appears on maps as far back as 1697, is
regularly demonstrated by a decoyman and a specially trained dog. The
decoy takes the form of a large funnel-shaped net-covered hoops set
along a channel, or 'pipe', off the lake. Alongside are thatched screens,
set at angles. The method is to exploit the ducks' defensive curiosity in
other creatures.

   The dogs used – Kooikerhondjes – a Dutch breed similar to a King
Charles spaniel – circles successive screens, thus drawing the ducks
farther and farther into the narrowing net funnel. Once the ducks have
been caught, they are ringed and returned to the wild so that their
movements can be studied. Open April-August Bank Holiday
(Tel: 0494 28051).

Places of Interest in the Neighbourhood
Civil War Stronghold (Boarstall)
Silence in Court (Long Crendon)
Robbers' Hideout (Oakley)

12 Civil War Stronghold

Position: Boarstall Tower (NT) is situated about 11 miles due W of
Aylesbury.
O.S. Map: Aylesbury area; Sheet 165; 1/50,000.
Map Ref: SP 624/141.
Access: Off B4011, from A41(T).

Only the huge gatehouse of the 14th-century Boarstall Castle, bounded
by a moat on three sides, survives; but what remains is very impressive,
especially from the gardens on the south side.

Now in the care of the National Trust, it was once owned by the
Aubrey family and was a stronghold of the Royalists in the Civil War
until its capture for Parliament in 1646.

The Royalists did much damage to Boarstall, and the church was
demolished and the village destroyed so as not to give cover to their
opponents. During the rest of the century, Boarstall was extensively
rebuilt.

Write to tenant for appointment to view the gatehouse, or telephone
09844 238201. (Information: 0494 28051.)

Places of Interest in the Neighbourhood
Out for the Ducks (Boarstall)
Robbers' Hideout (Oakley)
Silence in Court (Long Crendon)

Boarstall Castle's imposing medieval gateway.

The rescued Harvard KF435 at Booker Aircraft Museum.

13 Relics of the Air Wars

Position: Booker Aircraft Museum is in Wycombe Air Park, SW of
High Wycombe.
O.S. Map: Reading & Windsor area; Sheet 175; 1/50,000.
Map Ref: SU 831/907.
Access: Turn off B482 into Clay Lane, about 2 miles NW of Marlow,
for the airfield.

'Recover to remember' is the motto of this evocative and interesting
Museum. For many years David King, its founder, has been digging
up parts of old aircraft – among them engines, dashboard instruments and propeller blades – from German and Allied aircraft which
crashed during and after the Second World War. He and other aviation
archaeologists have garnered them from hundreds of sites all over
southern England, including the Chilterns, and many are on show. One
is a Hercules engine from a Wellington bomber that crashed near
Quainton.

King has been able to rescue some complete aircraft, including a
Vampire T11, Whirlwind HAR7, Harvard KF435, the cockpit sections
of a Canberra WJ789, DC3 and A26 Invader, and the noses of a
Jetstream and Javelin.

Older visitors will particularly appreciate the Museum's Home Front
section. On show are gas-masks for children – one of which completely
enclosed a baby – a Mickey Mouse gas-mask for slightly older children,
as well as a gas eye-shield and a leaflet advising what to do if the
invader came, and an ARP gas warning rattle.

From the First World War come a flying coat and helmet of 2/Lt G.
Osmond, Royal Flying Corps, who had been a member of the Ox and
Bucks Regt. There are also some relics from the crashed Flying Fortress
of Lt Clyde Cosper (see No 66, 'The Pilot who Saved a Town').

The Museum presents talks and slide shows on aviation archaeology,
and is open all the year at weekends (Tel: 0494 452320).

Places of Interest in the Neighbourhood
Sitting Pretty (High Wycombe)
In Praise of Women (High Wycombe)
Disraeli's Admirer (High Wycombe)

14 The 'Baby Saint'

Position: Buckingham is 8 miles W of Milton Keynes.
O.S. Map: Northampton & M. Keynes area; Sheet 152; 1/50,000.
Map Ref: SP 694/336.
Access: The Manor House stands near the junction of Church Street and Manor Street. No access into house.

High in the wall of this timbered Tudor house – the entrance hall was once the setting for Stowe manorial court – is a cherubic relief of the Anglo-Saxon 'baby saint' Rumbold. The child lived in the 7th century, and in the Middle Ages his shrine in Buckingham, on the site of the present church of St Peter and St Paul nearby, attracted many pilgrims.

   Rumbold's father was King of Northumbria, his mother was a daughter of Penda, King of Mercia. Immediately after his birth near Banbury in AD 623, he is supposed to have announced in a clear voice, 'I am a Christian', was baptised at his own request, then preached a sermon. He lived for only three days and died in King's Sutton, near Banbury. Eventually his body was taken to Buckingham.

Places of Interest in the Neighbourhood
Chantry Chapel (Buckingham)
Strongpoint of the Law (Buckingham)
The Biggest Garden of All (Stowe)

Rumbold, a precocious young saint.

28

15 Chantry Chapel

Position: Buckingham is 8 miles W of Milton Keynes.
O.S. Map: Northampton & M. Keynes area; Sheet 152; 1/50,000.
Map Ref: SP 693/340.
Access: The Chantry Chapel (NT) stands in Market Hill.

The Chantry Chapel of St John, claimed to be the town's oldest building, was rebuilt in 1475, but still features its fine Norman south door. It was rebuilt by Gilbert Scott in 1875, when in use as a Latin or Grammar School.

It is open from April to the end of October. Admission by written appointment with the Buckingham Heritage Trust, The Old Gaol, Market Hill, Buckingham MK18 1EW (Tel: 0296 382000).

Places of Interest in the Neighbourhood
Strongpoint of the Law (Buckingham)
Tribute to Florence (Middle Claydon)
The Biggest Garden of All (Stowe)

The Norman door to the Chantry Chapel.

16 Strongpoint of the Law

Position: Buckingham is 8 miles W of Milton Keynes.
O.S. Map: Northampton, M. Keynes area; Sheet 152; 1/50,000.
Map Ref: SP 698/343.
Access: The Old Gaol is between Market Hill and High Street.

This imposing gaol, planned as a mock castle, with battlements, turrets and trefoil windows, and looking just as forbidding, was built by the 1st Viscount Cobham in 1748 to help the town retain the Assizes (which in fact passed to Aylesbury).

   Despite its outward sturdy appearance, which adds much visual interest to the town, it had the reputation of being easy to escape from. One inmate walked straight out. Another, 'Scroggs' Wesley, made himself a noose rope out of strips of blanket, hauled himself up on the inside and then slid down the outside and fled.

   The Old Gaol is now a heritage centre and council offices.

Places of Interest in the Neighbourhood
Chantry Chapel (Buckingham)
Relics of Florence (Middle Claydon)
The Biggest Garden of All (Stowe)

The castle-like prison in Buckingham's town centre.

17 Men of Iron

Position: The Iron Age fort is in Bulstrode Park, near Gerrards Cross.
O.S. Map: Reading, Windsor area; Sheet 175; 1/50,000.
Map Ref: SU 995/880.
Access: From the A40 at Gerrards Cross, turn south into B416, turn
right into Camp Road and then left. There are several access points and
parking places.

Bulstrode Camp is a huge Iron Age earthworks, which encloses 22
acres. It is the largest of Buckinghamshire's many hillforts, and may
have been built by the Catuvellauni, a Celtic tribe who occupied the
area prior before the Roman Conquest.

Behind the trees which encircle the site is an almost continuous double
row of ditches and ramparts. The fort stands in the south-east corner of
Bulstrode Park, in which once stood a house largely rebuilt by the
notorious 'hanging judge', Judge Jeffreys. He lived there until his death
in 1689. The present house, which stands in grounds laid out by
Repton, was built in 1862.

Places of Interest in the Neighbourhood
It's a Small World (Beaconsfield)
Murders Most Foul (Denham)
Carry On Filming (Pinewood)

18 Death of 'His Majesty'

Position: Burnham Beeches is about 2 miles S of Beaconsfield.
O.S. Map: Reading, Windsor area; Sheet 175; 1/50,000.
Map Ref: SU 943/846.
Access: From M40 (Junction 2), then south along A355. Burnham
Beeches is immediately west.

> 'There at the foot of yonder nodding beech
> That wreaths its old fantastic roots so high
> His listless length at noontide would he stretch
> And pore upon the brook that babbles by.'

One would like to imagine that Thomas Gray's elegy was referring to
'His Majesty', the great-grandfather of trees in the magnificent 540
acres of Burnham Beeches. But the Swilly, 'the brook that babbles by',
was some distance from the ancient beech tree.

Until the freak storm of October 1987, to which it fell victim, 'His
Majesty' had stood for around 600 years. With a girth of 29ft 1 ins and
until then believed to be the largest and oldest pollarded tree in the
British Isles, it is now, alas, just a hulk.

In 1989, to mark the 800th year of the mayoralty of the City of London, the site was re-dedicated, and a replacement planted beside its
distinguished predecessor by the Lord Mayor, Sir Christopher Collett.

Like Epping Forest in Essex, Burnham Beeches is owned and
managed for the public by the Corporation of London, which bears all
costs from its 'Private Purse'. It is a site of special scientific interest, and
a mecca for naturalists of all kinds – from birdwatchers to botanists – as
well as the public who come to enjoy its peace. The composer Felix
Mendelssohn and the singer Jenny Lind used to walk and sit among the
Burnham beeches, and their favourite views are marked by plaques.

Burnham is a fine example of lopped beeches, whose average age has
been estimated at nearly 400 years. Pollarding was the ancient practice
of lopping the top of a tree above head height, enabling new shoots to
grow beyond the reach of grazing animals. The cut branches were used
for fodder and fuel.

Places of Interest in the Neighbourhood
It's a Small World (Beaconsfield)
Riverside Grandeur (Cliveden)
Men of Iron (Gerrards Cross)

19 From Coaching Days

Position: Chalfont Common, 3 miles E of High Wycombe.
O.S. Map: North & West London; Sheet 176; 1/50,000.
Map Ref: SU 003/924.
Access: The obelisk is at the junction of Monument and Chesham Lanes.

This stocky obelisk, erected in 1785 by Sir Henry Gott near Chalfont St Peter, commemorates the killing on that spot of a stag by George III. Well above head level is a plaque bearing distances – presumably for the use of coachmen, who would see them sitting high on their driving seats:

> To Newland I mile III furlongs; To Chesham VII.
> Built by Sir H. T. Gott; restored by W. Brown 1879.
> To Denham IV miles; to Uxbridge VI miles; London XXI.

Places of Interest in the Neighbourhood
Buildings on the Move (Chalfont St Giles)
Paradise Conserved (Chalfont St Giles)
Return of the Mayflower (Jordans)

Milestone memorial, where George III killed a stag.

20   Buildings on the Move

Position: Chalfont St Giles is E of High Wycombe.
O.S. Map: West London area; Sheet 176; 1/50,000.
Map Ref: TQ 010/940.
Access: Chiltern Open Air Museum is in Newland Park, off Gorelands
Lane.

For many years, staff of the Chiltern Open Air Museum have been
transporting and reassembling, brick by brick, on this 45-acre site,
local buildings that would otherwise have been demolished and lost

A reconstructed Iron Age hut at Chiltern Open Air Museum.

from view. Collectively, these relics demonstrate a way of life from a past age.

Included among the authentic buildings (one or two are reconstructions) are a shepherd's spartan living van, granary, forge and a 19th-century farmstead, including barns and stables and privy, a turn-of-the-century public convenience, some late 18th-century cottages and a 1950s telephone box. High Wycombe's brick-built crenellated toll-house, dating back to 1826, also has a new life as a museum feature.

The most impressive of the reconstructions is the Iron Age house, based on evidence from excavations near Dunstable – a large conical-shaped structure of thatch, intended for a family, furnished as it would have been in 150 BC, with 'kitchen' fire, pots and spit, and with no means for the smoke to escape except by filtering through the thatched roof. There is also a wooden bed-frame, with sheepskin and hay covering the floor – the kind of thing one would expect, we are told, in a typical comfortable, upper-class home of that period.

Buildings are continually being added to the display. Among the newcomers is a 1947 'prefab' – an inexpensive type of one-storey house erected after World War II.

A nature trail through a bluebell wood and chalk pits helps to demonstrate the benefits of woodland coppicing. The Museum is open April-October (Tel: 0494 871117).

Places of Interest in the Neighbourhood
The Gentle Giants (Chalfont St Giles)
Paradise Conserved (Chalfont St Giles)
From Coaching Days (Chalfont Common)

21 Paradise Conserved

Position: Chalfont St Giles is 4 miles E of High Wycombe.
O.S. Map: Reading & Windsor area; Sheet 175; 1/50,000.
Map Ref: SU 988/933.
Access: Milton's Cottage is on the S side of High Street

The poet John Milton fled the Great Plague in London in 1665 and, at
the suggestion of a friend, the Quaker Thomas Ellwood, rented this
beautiful low-ceilinged 16th-century timbered cottage. As a fervent
supporter of the Parliamentary cause during the Civil War, Milton was
for a time Latin Secretary to the Protector, Cromwell, in London. After
the Restoration of the monarchy in 1660, he became disillusioned,
moved to Chalfont and completed his great work 'Paradise Lost'.

When shown it by Milton, Ellwood said: 'Thou hast said much here of
Paradise Lost . But what has thou to say of Paradise Found '? The
result was Milton's second great work, 'Paradise Regained'.

Milton's Cottage, which is administered by a trust, contains a number
of relics and artefacts, including a lock of the poet's hair, first editions
of both poems, portraits and busts of the poet, a visitors' book of a
century ago, and a letter sent on Queen Victoria's behalf, promising £20
towards the cost of buying the cottage. The Cottage is open March–
October (Tel: 02407 2313).

Places of Interest in the Neighbourhood
Buildings on the Move (Chalfont St Giles)
The Gentle Giants (Chalfont St Giles)
From Coaching Days (Chalfont Common)

22 Scene of the Crime

Position: Cheddington is 4 miles S of Leighton Buzzard.
O.S. Map: Aylesbury area; Sheet 165; 1/50,000.
Map Ref: SP 917/208.
Access: Railway bridge No 127 is a few yards off B488, at signpost left
to Mentmore, Ledburn and Wing, 2 miles north of the village.

On August 9, 1963, the newspapers reported one of the biggest and
most audacious crimes of all time – the Great Train Robbery, which
took place at this bridge.

After months of planning, a gang of 15 men, armed and wearing
masks, altered the signals, stopped a night mail train travelling south
from Leighton Buzzard, and made off with 2.6 million pounds in notes
due to be destroyed.

At precisely 3.10 am, the train was stopped, the driver and fireman
made to uncouple the engine and front two coaches, which were driven
up the line to this bridge. The Post Office sorting staff were over-
powered, and the train robbers unloaded the mailbags down the bank
to the right of the bridge (pictured here) to where the rest of the gang
was waiting with three vehicles. They bundled the bags into these and
drove off to Leatherslade Farm at Oakley (see No 60, 'The Robbers'
Hide-Out').

At the scene of the crime, police found a brown glove, which the gang

*The train robbers unloaded their haul down the slope to the right of this
bridge at Cheddington.*

had used to black out the green light, and some torch batteries which lit up the red one.

No-one was able to give the alarm for half an hour. Train driver Jack Mills and fireman David Whitby were both badly beaten up and could not summon help because the telephone wires had been cut.

More than any other modern crime, the Great Train Robbery caught the public's imagination for its scale and daring, and inspired several books and films. Men such as Buster Edwards and Ronald Biggs were seen as heroes rather than the villains they were.

Places of Interest in the Neighbourhood
Old Mill by the Stream (Ivinghoe)
In Case of Fire (Ivinghoe)
Down on the Ancient Farm (Pitstone)

The chimneys at Chenies copied by Henry VIII.

23 An Unfaithful Queen

Position: Chenies village is a mile NW of Chorleywood.
O.S. Map: Luton & Hertford area; Sheet 166; 1/50,000.
Map Ref: TQ 015/984.
Access: Drive from village leads to Chenies Manor.

There was one thing that Henry VIII, a frequent visitor to Chenies
Manor, took away with him after his stay – the design of those
ornamental chimneys which became a characteristic architectural
feature of the Tudor period. In fact, when Henry rebuilt Hampton
Court, the exquisite craftsmanship on the chimneys was repeated by the
same workmen who had built the Tudor wing at Chenies.

For centuries a property of the Russell family, the Earls and Dukes of
Bedford, Chenies is full of interest. One of Henry VIII's wives, the
ill-fated Kathryn Howard, committed adultery here with her cousin,
Thomas Culpepper, and both were later executed.

According to the present owners, Lt-Col Alistair and Elizabeth
MacLeod Matthews, who have lived here since the 1950s, the noise of a
'heavy limping tread' can sometimes be heard on the staircase and
along the passage to Kathryn's bedroom. Henry suffered from an
ulcerated leg, and tradition has it that his ghost stumps through the
house checking up on the suspect behaviour of his wife.

Among many curiosities in Chenies Manor are a 13th-century stone
crypt, once reputedly used as a wine cellar by Edward I; a Tudor privy,
off what is now the library; a room where Queen Elizabeth I is thought
to have held court; and an impressive collection of antique dolls and
prams in one of the bedrooms. Chenies Manor is open April-October
(Tel: 0494 762888).

Places of Interest in the Neighbourhood
Martyrs' Memorial (Amersham)
Paradise Conserved (Chalfont St Giles)
Honour for a Horse (Latimer)

24 Puddingstone Church

Position: Chesham is just N of Amersham.
O.S. Map: Aylesbury area; Sheet 165; 1/50,000.
Map Ref: SP 957/015.
Access: St Mary's Church is in Church Street.

How many admirers of the Gothic beauty of St Mary's Church trouble
to take a close look at the unusual bases to the buttresses on its south
side? These buttresses stand on lumps of a rare natural rock called
'puddingstone', which is found largely in neighbouring Hertfordshire,
but also in Buckinghamshire. At Chesham Bois it was used to line
tracks, and examples can be seen in the drive from Bois Lane to the
church.

At first glance, puddingstone resembles concrete. Lapidarists use
small pieces of the aggregate for ornaments and jewellery because it can
take a high polish. The Romans used it in their homes for rotary querns
– millstones for grinding corn – and whetstones.

Puddingstone is so called because of its resemblance to plum pudding.
It is a conglomerate made up of coloured flint pebbles – black, brown,
red, yellow, pink and orange – up to two inches across, set in a hard
natural silica cement. It was formed 60 million years ago from the
pebble beds which were deposited when the sea withdrew from south-
east England. When the sea returned, it brought with it material that
produced the 'cement' that binds it. Then the beds rose to form dry
land.

Dowsing rods react to puddingstone as they do to water, but no-one
can explain why.

Places of Interest in the Neighbourhood
Martyrs' Memorial (Amersham)
An Unfaithful Queen (Chenies)
Liberty's Ship (The Lee)

Puddingstone bases support the porch at Chesham church.

25 Tribute to Florence

Position: Claydon House (NT) is at Middle Claydon, 5 miles S of Buckingham.
O.S. Map: Aylesbury area; Sheet 165; 1/50,000.
Map Ref: SP 720/253.
Access: Along the drive from the village.

A frequent guest at Claydon House, a National Trust property since 1956, was Florence Nightingale. Her sister Parthenope was married to Sir Harry Verney, one of the Verney family which owned it, and she spent many of her summers there.

In the museum next to Florence's bedroom (containing portraits of her) there is some memorabilia of 'the Lady with the Lamp', notably letters. One is from Queen Victoria, enclosing a brooch 'to commemorate your great and blessed work, and which I hope you will wear as a mark of the high approbation of your sovereign'.

One of the Verneys, Sir Francis, was a pirate. In addition to his portrait, there is a large glass case on show containing his robe, cap and slippers, mulberry coloured and worked in gold thread.

For any admirer of rococo work, this house is a study in the style. The white-painted woodwork by Lightfoot and plasterwork by Rose are at their most extravagant here. Visitors should remember to look up, as well as around them, for the ceilings as well as the walls offer the most tasteful displays of plasterwork. Lightfoot's chinoiserie style reaches its peak in the Chinese room on the first floor.

The Verneys originally came into possession of land here in 1471. The manor house built in the 16th century was enlarged by the 2nd Earl in the middle of the 18th, and parts of it were demolished in the 19th, when a new south front was built. There is a 17th-century Gothic pavilion in the grounds.

Sir Edmund Verney, who was standard-bearer to Charles I, was killed at the Battle of Edgehill in 1642. The story goes that, after the battle, his severed hand was found still gripping the Royal Standard.

Places of Interest in the Neighbourhood
Chantry Chapel (Buckingham)
Stronghold of the Law (Buckingham)
Getting Steamed Up (Quainton)

26 Riverside Grandeur

Position: On the E bank of the Thames, just N of Taplow.
O.S. Map: Reading, Windsor area; Sheet 175; 1/50,000.
Map Ref: SU 910/853.
Access: Cliveden (NT) is off Cliveden Road leading N from Taplow.

Cliveden's Thames-side house and grounds are as famous, sometimes as notorious, as some of the people associated with it and its wealthy owners, the Astors. There were the Astors' influential 'Cliveden Set' before the Second World War and, later, the events surrounding the Profumo scandal of the early 1960s. It is now a hotel (open for part of the year) owned by the National Trust.

The first house on this site was erected by the 2nd Duke of Buckingham in the 17th century. The present one was built in 1850-51 by Sir Charles Barry, who to a large extent maintained the shape and

Distant view of Cliveden from the Shell Fountain.

character of the previous one. It is generally regarded as a masterpiece. The Shell Fountain at the far end of the long Grand Avenue leading down to the house, sets the style for the formal gardens, which are scattered with sarcophagi, pavilions, amphitheatre, fountains, and smaller gardens with various themes, including roses, water and a war memorial.

In 1942 the house and gardens were given by the 2nd Viscount Astor and his wife Nancy (who became the first woman MP) to the National Trust. They continued living there until his death in 1952. The 3rd Viscount also lived in the house until 1966, when the Astors gave it up as the family home. The hotel and grounds are open to visitors March to end of December; house, April-October. (Tel: 0628 605069.)

Places of Interest in the Neighbourhood
It's a Small World (Beaconsfield)
Death of 'His Majesty' (Burnham Beeches)
Brunel's Feat – or Folly? (Taplow)

27 Once an MP . . .

Position: The Chiltern Hundreds, which include Stoke, Desborough
and Burnham, curve down from High Wycombe towards Slough.

That a Member of Parliament who wants to resign has to seek appointment as Steward of the Chiltern Hundreds is one of those oddities with
which Parliamentary tradition is charmingly besprinkled.

It arises from the time-honoured principle in English parliamentary
law that an MP, once elected, cannot resign his seat. So what can he do,
in order to leave Parliament between elections? The answer is to apply
to become Steward of the Chiltern Hundreds, who was a paid officer
originally appointed to protect inhabitants of the Chilterns against
robbers.

The Succession to the Crown Act of 1707 provided that every member
accepting an office of profit from the Crown should vacate his seat.
Eight crown stewardships were created to enable members to resign,
but only two survive: the offices of steward or bailiff of the three
Chiltern Hundreds of Stoke, Desborough and Burnham, and of the
manor of Northstead (in Yorkshire).

28 Chilterns High Spot

Position: Coombe Hill (NT) is a mile SW of Wendover.
O.S. Map: Aylesbury area; Sheet 165; 1/50,000.
Map Ref: SP 849/066.
Access: Take A4010 NE from Princes Risborough, turn right along
B4010, turn right towards Dunsmore after crossroads to bend in the
road; park and walk a few hundred yards to monument.

Near the top of Coombe Hill, at 852 feet one of the high points of the
Chilterns, is a granite monument commemorating the men of Buckinghamshire who lost their lives in the Boer War. Erected in 1904, it was
almost completely destroyed by lightning in 1938, but was rebuilt by
Buckinghamshire County Council soon afterwards.

There are impressive views from here. The OS triangulation point
bears an interesting metal plaque noting many landmarks visible on a
clear day, including Brill Hill (13 miles), the Cotswold Hills (55),
Aylesbury Church (5) and Chequers Court, the Prime Minister's
country home (three-quarters of a mile).

Places of Interest in the Neighbourhood
Prime Ministers' Retreat (Ellesborough)
Crosses in Chalk (Princes Risborough)
The Pilot Who Saved a Town (Princes Risborough)

The Boer War monument on Coombe Hill in the Chilterns.

29 Murders Most Foul

Position: Old Denham village is about 2 miles E of Gerrards Cross.
O.S. Map: North-West London; Sheet 176; 1/50,000.
Map Ref: SP 043/870.
Access: Turn off the A40 to Old Denham village. The church is in
Village Road.

Beneath the large stone slab about 40 yards to the right along the path
into this peaceful churchyard lie the victims of a brutal attack that
wiped out a whole family. One day last century, the village blacksmith
and six members of his family, including three children, were all axed to
death.

The victims were: Emmanuel Marshall, aged 35, the blacksmith, his
wife Charlotte (31), his 77-year-old mother Mary; his sister Mary Ann
(due to be married two days after the murders); and his children, Mary
(8), Tharaza (6) and Gertrude (4). They died in their cottage in nearby
Cheapside Lane on May 22, 1870.

The family were murdered for the most trivial of reasons: the
murderer, John Jones (alias Owen), an itinerant who had for a time
worked for Emmanuel Marshall, was resentful because he had broken a
hammer and the blacksmith had stopped the cost of it from his wages.

Although communications were rudimentary at the time, the police
worked swiftly to catch the murderer. Aided by a man who had met
Jones, they were soon on the trail through Uxbridge to Reading, where
he was caught in a lodging house. Less than three months later Jones
was convicted and hanged.

Places of Interest in the Neighbourhood
Men of Iron (Bulstrode Park)
Paradise Conserved (Chalfont St Giles)

30 Folly of Sir John

Position: Dinton is about three miles SW of Aylesbury.
O.S. Map: Aylesbury area; Sheet 165; 1/50,000.
Map Ref: SP 765/115.
Access: Dinton Castle folly is on N side of A418, a short walk from junction with Cuddington Road.

Don't be fooled by Dinton Castle's rather eerie ambiance, which certainly does not arise from any genuine hauntings. The castle is a ruined folly – originally much higher – with turrets, and now suitably overgrown with ivy. It was erected by Sir John Vanhatten in 1769 who wanted it as a setting for displaying his collection of fossils. Many of these – mostly large ammonites, the whirligig precursors of the snail – can be seen cemented into the walls.

Places of Interest in the Neighbourhood
When Hampden Said No (Aylesbury)
Evergreen Response (Aylesbury)
Gone to the Walls (Haddenham)

Dinton's Castle ruin with fossils in the walls.

31 The 'UFO' of 1871

Position: Downley lies on the N side of High Wycombe.
O.S. Map: Reading & Windsor area; Sheet 175; 1/50,000.
Map Ref: SU 848/944.
Access: Plomer Hill runs NE from West Wycombe Road.

In 1871, a much respected local builder and undertaker, William Loosley – who carried out work for Disraeli at Hughenden – claimed to have seen a UFO on or around Plomer Hill. In his detailed report of the incident in 'An Account of a Meeting with Denizens of Another World', Loosley describes how on the night of October 4th, feeling feverish and sleepless, he stood in his garden after midnight and noticed a star in motion – 'no mere shooting star', but one, he said, that moved with slow deliberation in 'wandering, questing fashion'. It settled over 'Plummers Green', coming down to earth looking a 'steady, unearthly white'.

Later, by day, he tramped across to Littleworth and 'Plummers Green' from his home and shop on the Oxford Road, and discovered a movement in the bushes nearby. Poking about with his stick, he came upon a metal-cased craft which moved with whirrings and lurchings. He writes of a strange white globe which hung in the air, and hoops with globes at their centre which appeared and disappeared. At one stage Loosley was prompted to observe: 'Sirs, your conjurer's show is all a mystery to me'.

It remains a mystery. Fourteen years after this bizarre experience, in 1885, Loosley noted wonderingly: 'It now seems that pictures that move and counterfeit life can be contrived by machinery... images which move in every respect by some clever trickery' – obviously a reference to the forerunners of movie film, then being seen. So did Loosley really see what he claimed, or was it all a product of his feverish imagination?

Loosley died in 1893. He is buried in the family grave in section C of Wycombe Cemetery.

Places of Interest in the Neighbourhood
Happy Genius (Downley)
In Praise of Women (High Wycombe)
Disraeli's Admirer (High Wycombe)

32 Happy Genius

Position: The monument to Disraeli's father is near Downley, N of High Wycombe.
O.S. Map: Reading & Windsor area; Sheet 175; 1/50,000.
Map Ref: SU 857/946.
Access: A4128 northwards from High Wycombe for half a mile, left up Coates Lane, left to Wyndhams Avenue, then along footpath skirting Tinkers Wood (NT).

This stone monument, on a hillside above Hughenden Manor, commemorates Isaac, father of the Victorian Prime Minister Benjamin

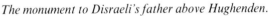

The monument to Disraeli's father above Hughenden.

Disraeli, 1st Earl of Beaconsfield. It was erected in 1862 by Mary Anne, Benjamin's wife, 'in affectionate remembrance' of Isaac, 'who, by his happy genius diffused among the multitude that elevating taste for literature which before his time was the privilege only of the learned'.

Isaac D'Israeli wrote books of literary and historical anecdotes, of which the best-known was *Curiosities of Literature*. The first volume was published in 1791, with subsequent ones in 1793 and 1817. He also wrote some histories and several novels.

His son Benjamin wrote of him: 'His feelings, though always amiable, were not painfully deep, and amid joy or sorrow the philosophic vein was ever evident'.

Places of Interest in the Neighbourhood
The 'UFO' of 1871 (Downley)
Sitting Pretty (High Wycombe)
In Praise of Women (High Wycombe)

Chequers Court, a gift to the nation.

33 Prime Ministers' Retreat

Position: Chequers is near Ellesborough, SW of Wendover.
O.S. Map: Aylesbury area; Sheet 165; 1/50,000.
Map Ref: SP 842/057.
Access: No access to the house, which is visible in the distance from
Coombe Hill (see 'Chilterns High Spot').

It seems fitting that John Hampden's blow for parliamentary
democracy by publicly declaring refusal to pay Ship Money to Charles I
should have been made barely a mile away. For it is near Ellesborough
that the leaders of parliamentary democracy, the Prime Ministers, have
a permanent country home.

   Lord Lee of Fareham, who lived in Chequers Court, made the house
his gift to the nation for the purpose in 1917, with the funds to maintain
it. An inscription in the house reads:

> This house of peace and ancient memories was given
> to England as a thank-offering for her deliverance in
> the Great War and as a place of rest and recreation
> for her Prime Ministers for ever.

Places of Interest in the Neighbourhood
Chilterns High Spot (Coombe Hill)
The Pilot Who Saved a Town (Princes Risborough)
Crosses in Chalk (Princes Risborough)

34 Tower with Two Roofs

Position: Fingest is about 3 miles W of High Wycombe.
O.S. Map: Reading & Windsor area; Sheet 175; 1/50,000.
Map Ref: SU 777/912.
Access: Off B482 at Bolter End, 4 miles NW of Marlow.

Pevsner describes the Norman tower of St Bartholomew's Church at Fingest as 'rightly famous' but 'absurdly mighty for the church appended to it'. It is enormously strong – 60 feet high and about 27 feet square with walls four feet thick – although the double-gabled saddleback roof was added later, probably in the 17th century.

The Manor of Fingest was at one time held by the Bishops of Lincoln (the area being then in Lincoln diocese). One of them was a villainous Henry Burgwash, whose ghost is said to haunt local common land – which he is supposed to have stolen from Fingest villagers, reducing them to poverty.

The ghost of this hated man is reportedly seen dressed as a forester, with bow, quiver and horn. Those who meet him are told it is his eternal punishment to be keeper of the land he stole. Should the Canons of Lincoln be asked to restore the land to its rightful owners, the Bishop's ghost will be laid.

One of Fingest's distinguished residents was Sir William Connor, the one-time *Daily Mirror* columnist 'Cassandra', who became famous for his acerbic essays.

Places of Interest in the Neighbourhood
Relic of Wolsey (Hambledon)
In Praise of Women (High Wycombe)
Sitting Pretty (High Wycombe)

The rare saddleback church tower at Fingest.

35 A Standard of Loyalty

Position: Forty Green, western edge of Beaconsfield.
O.S. Map: Reading & Windsor area; Sheet 175; 1/50,000.
Map Ref: SU 923/919.
Access: From E side of road from Beaconsfield to Penn.

The old inn, The Royal Standard of England, can trace its history back to the Norman Conquest, when it was called The Ship. How it changed its name is a proud story.

After his defeat by Cromwell at the Battle of Worcester in 1651, Charles II escaped and sheltered at The Ship during his six weeks' flight. Only 50 people, including the landlord, knew the King's whereabouts, and not one of them betrayed him, even though £1,000 – a huge sum in those days – was offered for information leading to his capture.

Following the Restoration and his triumphant return to the throne in 1660, Charles II, not forgetting that the good people of Forty Green had saved his life, authorised the inn's name to be changed to 'The Royal Standard of England' – a name borne by no other hostelry in the country.

The King sheltered in a room above what is called King Charles's Bar.

Places of Interest in the Neighbourhood
It's a Small World (Beaconsfield)
Men of Iron (Gerrards Cross)
Return of the Mayflower (Jordans)

36 Gone to the Walls

Position: Haddenham is about 2 miles NE of Thame.
O.S. Map: Aylesbury area; Sheet 165; 1/50,000.
Map Ref: SP 742/081.
Access: Wichert-made walls can be seen everywhere in the old village area.

Several villages in this south-west corner of Buckinghamshire use wichert, a kind of chalk mixed with straw, as a building material. It covers many walls in Haddenham, Cuddington and Lower Winchendon.

   Haddenham is said to possess the best examples of wichert, concentrated in the old village area in the south. Boundary walls are almost invariably topped by a row of red pantiles, to protect the wichert from crumbling. The wise owner has them faced with a more durable material.

   The Bone House (built in 1807), in the High Street, half a mile from

The Bone House, in the High Street at Haddenham.

the old village, has a facade easily seen from the street. The house's walls are adorned with all manner of designs and patterns formed out of the knucklebones of sheep – human faces, spades and forks and hearts among them.

Places of Interest in the Neighbourhood
When Hampden Said No (Aylesbury)
Silence in Court (Long Crendon)
The Pilot Who Saved a Town (Princes Risborough)

The oaken Wolsey Altar in Hambleden church.

37 Relic of Wolsey

Position: Hambleden is about 3 miles W of Marlow.
O.S. Map: Reading & Windsor area; Sheet 175; 1/50,000.
Map Ref: SU 784/865.
Access: The church is in the village centre.

The oaken altar in the south transept, dating from about 1520, is
known as the Wolsey Altar. The panelling was formerly a bed-head
which is believed to have belonged to the Sandys family, who lived near
Basingstoke, where Wolsey, Bishop Fox and Henry VIII were regular
visitors.

It came to Hambleden, it is thought, through the marriage of Henry
Sandys's widow Elizabeth to Ralph Scrope, of a local family, a member
of whom, Adrian, was a signatory to Charles I's death warrant.

The Lady Chapel, which was previously known as the Sheepfold, once
had wooden benches and straw on the floor for the use of smocked
farm-workers. It was beatified in 1914 in memory of W. H. Smith MP –
whose father was the founder of W. H. Smith & Son – and his wife Lady
Hambleden. They are buried just inside the entrance to Hambleden
Cemetery.

After various posts under Disraeli, W. H. Smith MP occupied Walmer
Castle as Warden of the Cinque Ports. He died at Walmer in 1891, and
in recognition of his services his widow was ennobled in her own right,
as the 1st Viscountess Hambleden.

The 7th Earl of Cardigan, who led the Light Brigade to catastrophe at
Balaklava in 1854, was born in the village. His oak chest stands near the
fine D'Oyley family monument.

Places of Interest in the Neighbourhood
Tower with Two Roofs (Fingest)
Twinge of Gout (Marlow)
Frankenstein's Birthplace (Marlow)

38 Unknown Warriors

Position: Hardwick is about 2 miles N of Aylesbury.
O.S. Map: Aylesbury area; Sheet 165; 1:50,000.
Map Ref: SP 806/190.
Access: St Mary's Church is on the E side of the A413.

Below the tower outside St Mary's Church is a tomb containing the remains of 247 Civil War soldiers who were killed in battle. They were discovered in 1818 buried in a field adjoining Holman's Bridge, across the Thame on the A413 on the northern edge of Aylesbury (map ref SP 818/154). This was the scene of an engagement in 1642 between the Charles I's troops commanded by Prince Rupert and the Parliamentary troops who held Aylesbury. The tomb was erected by the late Lord Nugent.

Places of Interest in the Neighbourhood
When Hampden Said No (Aylesbury)
Sitting Pretty (Aylesbury)
Birthplace of Mrs Miniver (Whitchurch)

Where hundreds of Civil War soldiers are buried at Hardwick.

39 Sitting Pretty

Position: Wycombe Local History and Chair Museum is on the E side
of High Wycombe.
O.S. Map: Reading, Windsor area; Sheet 175; 1:50,000.
Map Ref: SU 868/933.
Access: Just N of High Wycombe station (BR), take Priory Road off
Amersham Hill, left into Priory Avenue.

One of the area's traditional staple industries, the making of Windsor
chairs, is generously featured in the Wycombe Chair Museum. The
exhibition is divided into three parts: chair making as a craft, tools of
the trade, and a history of the craft.

Windsor chairs have been made in the area for more than 250 years. A

A chair display at High Wycombe Museum.

little under a century ago there were 50 chairmakers in Wycombe, with many others in surrounding villages. They used foot-operated lathes, which became power-operated with the coming of factories during the Industrial Revolution. There were only a few of these in 1800; by 1860 they had increased to 150.

The industry attracted some large commissions. In 1873 there was one for 19,000 chairs for a Moody and Sankey evangelical meeting, and the Crystal Palace ordered another 8,000.

Ercol, the well-known furniture company, has continued the chair-making tradition, and demonstrates, in its own exhibition, how the processes once carried out by hand are now done by machine, without sacrificing quality.

Places of Interest in the Neighbourhood
The 'UFO' of 1871 (Downley)
In Praise of Women (High Wycombe)
Relics of the Air Wars (High Wycombe)

The Women's Window in All Saints Church.

40 In Praise of Women

Position: All Saints Church is in High Wycombe.
O.S. Map: Reading, Windsor area; Sheet 175; 1:50,000.
Map Ref: SU 865/934.
Access: From Church Street.

In the north transept of All Saints Church is a modern stained-glass window which pays tribute to the role of women in ministering to others.

It was given by Dame Frances Dove, who made her mark in several ways: as founder of Wycombe Abbey School (in 1896) and its head-mistress until 1910, as a pioneer of a child welfare clinic as early as 1908, and as Wycombe's first woman town councillor. In the last role she ran up against popular prejudice and was denied being made mayor of the town. There is a pointed irony in the placing of her window: it is visible from where the mayor usually sits during services.

Women who figure in the window are: Queen Victoria, Grace Darling, Emily Bronte, Mary Slessor, Christina Rossetti, Elizabeth Fry, Florence Nightingale, Margaret Godolphin, Emily Davies, Margaret Roper, Margaret Beaufort, Alice Marval, and Saints Bridget, Frideswide, Hilda, Margaret and Winefred.

Dame Frances, who died in 1942, is buried in section C1 of Wycombe Cemetery.

Places of Interest in the Neighbourhood
The 'UFO' of 1871 (Downley)
Sitting Pretty (High Wycombe)
Weighed Down with Work? (High Wycombe)

41 Weighed Down with Work?

Position: High Wycombe Guildhall.
O.S. Map: Reading & Windsor area; Sheet 175; 1:50,000.
Map Ref: SU 865/930.
Access: Junction of High Street and Pauls Row.

A ceremony thought to date from medieval times takes place in mid-May every year at the ancient Guildhall, when the retiring mayor, the in-coming mayor and all the councillors and officers are weighed and the result announced by the town crier.

Any weight increase shown is greeted with jeers and boos; no gain and there are cheers and claps. Any weight gain during the year in office is lightheartedly taken to be the result of growing fat at the ratepayers' expense; any weight loss is put down to hard work in their interests.

One local legend attributes the weighing-in to a visit of Queen Elizabeth I to Wycombe in 1566 on the day of the election of a new mayor (at Michaelmas). Surprised and suspicious at the corpulence of the Mayor and Corporation, she ordered that they should be weighed.

Brass jockey scales that once appeared at fetes and fairs are used at the ceremony. Wycombe's heaviest mayor was Councillor Roy Wood, who tipped the scales at a remarkable 20st 5lbs in 1960.

Places of Interest in the Neighbourhood
The 'UFO' of 1871 (Downley)
Sitting Pretty (High Wycombe)
In Praise of Women (High Wycombe)

An old photograph of the Mayor of High Wycombe being weighed.

Disraeli family graves and that of Mrs Brydges-Williams.

42 Disraeli's Admirer

Position: Hughenden Manor (NT), N of High Wycombe.
O.S. Map: Aylesbury area; Sheet 165; 1:50,000.
Map Ref: SU 866/955.
Access: Coming from High Wycombe, turn up drive on left, a mile or two along A4128.

Outside the eastern end of the church in the grounds of Benjamin Disraeli's home at Hughenden Manor is the family vault, with four panels stating who is buried there. In the first, third and fourth are Disraeli and his wife Mary Anne, his brothers, and their children.

Who then is the mysterious Mrs Sarah Brydges-Willyams named on the second panel? The strange answer is that this elderly widow, an admirer of Disraeli, paid to be buried there. Disraeli, a leading politician, later Chancellor of the Exchequer and Prime Minister as well as a noted author, was nevertheless always short of money, and when Mrs Brydges-Williams offered him £30,000 if she could be buried beside him, Disraeli felt he could only accept it.

Another admirer of Disraeli was Queen Victoria. The inscription on the memorial to him in the church reads: 'This memorial is placed by his grateful Sovereign and Friend Victoria RI. Kings love him that speaketh right – Proverbs XVI 13'.

Hughenden Manor is a three-storey Georgian brick building, and is where Disraeli and his wife went to live in 1848 when he was already a successful novelist and leader of the Tories in the House of Commons. He became 1st Earl of Beaconsfield in 1876.

Visitors can tour Hughenden's grounds, and in the house see Dizzy's study, which is still much as it was in his day. Memorabilia includes the original manuscript of *Coningsby* and his quill pen.

Open April to end October (Tel: 0494 32580).

Places of Interest in the Neighbourhood
The 'UFO' of 1871 (Downley)
Sitting Pretty (High Wycombe)
In Praise of Women (High Wycombe)

43 A Rare Dovecote

Position: Horsenden village is just SW of Princes Risborough.
O.S. Map: Aylesbury area; Sheet 165; 1:50,000.
Map Ref: SP 794/029.
Access: From Horsenden Road. Although on private premises, the dovecote is clearly visible from the public footpath by the thatched cottage opposite drive to the Horsenden Manor.

A delightful and very handsome dovecote is to be seen not far from the church in the tranquil hamlet of Horsenden. It is made of timber and said to date from 1550, though it has been restored. It has a pyramid roof, with nesting places for doves on the upper floor, surmounted by another, smaller pyramid.

Places of Interest in the Neighbourhood
Chilterns High Spot (Wendover)
The Pilot Who Saved a Town (Princes Risborough)
Crosses in Chalk (Princes Risborough and Bledlow)

The 16th-century dovecote at Horsenden.

44 In Case of Fire . . .

Position: Ivinghoe is 5 miles S of Leighton Buzzard.
O.S. Map: Aylesbury area; Sheet 165; 1/50,000.
Map Ref: SP 946/162.
Access: The thatch hook hangs along the church wall in Church Road.

When village homes were roofed largely with thatch, fire was an
ever-present danger. A relic and reminder of those days is on the church
boundary wall in Ivinghoe village: an 18ft-long hook, used to tear
thatch from burning cottages, dating back to the 18th century. Beneath
it is another reminder of the ruthless way they had with poachers: an
iron mantrap.

There is a tradition that Ivinghoe village lent its name to the hero
of Sir Walter Scott's book *Ivanhoe*, published in 1819. Perhaps Scott
picked up the name from the local verse that was around at that time:

> Tring, Wing and Ivanhoe
> Hampden of Hampden did forgo
> For striking of ye Prince a blow
> And glad he might escapen so.

Places of Interest in the Neighbourhood
Point of View (Ivinghoe)
Old Mill by the Stream (Ivinghoe)
Down on the Ancient Farm (Pitstone)

Firefighting relic, an 18ft long thatch hook at Ivinghoe.

45 Point of View

Position: Ivinghoe Beacon is 5 miles S of Leighton Buzzard.
O.S. Map: Aylesbury area; Sheet 165; 1/50,000.
Map Ref: SP 961/169.
Access: From B489, a mile NE of Ivinghoe village.

Ivinghoe Beacon, 807 feet high and only 30 miles from London, once helped to alert England to the approach of the Spanish Armada at the time of Queen Elizabeth I, when a network of fires was lit on hilltops throughout the country.

The Beacon, which marks one end of the Ridgeway Path – the other is at Avebury – is a favourite spot to enjoy the fine views on a clear day into the neighbouring Hertfordshire and Bedfordshire. The panorama is particularly impressive through a 90-degree arc from north-west to north-east, which takes in the Vale of Aylesbury.

On top of Beacon Hill is a triangular six-acre Iron Age hillfort with a ditch, and within this is a barrow, thought to date from the Bronze Age.

Places of Interest in the Neighbourhood
Scene of the Crime (Cheddington)
Old Mill by the Stream (Ivinghoe)
Down on the Ancient Farm (Pitstone)

46 Return of the *Mayflower*

Position: Jordans is 2 miles E of Beaconsfield.
O.S. Map: Reading, Windsor area; Sheet 175; 1/50,000.
Map Ref: SU 978/910.
Access: The Mayflower Barn stands in the grounds of the Old Jordans Quaker Guest House. Visitors must call first at the guest house and ask for admission.

No barn in Britain has such historic overtones as this one at Jordans: its oak timbers are believed to be those of the *Mayflower*, the ship that sailed with the Pilgrim Fathers from Plymouth to the New World of America in 1620.

Evidence for the claim includes a report by a Port of London marine surveyor that the barn was of early 17th-century origin and that its size – 90 ft by 20 ft wide – and probable weight corresponded to that of the

Graves of the Penn family at Jordans.

Mayflower, which was broken up at Rotherhithe, on the Thames, in 1624.

The Quaker antiquarian Rendel Harris noted that the barn had a cracked middle beam, just as the Mayflower had; and it is thought to have the name Harwich (port of registry of the *Mayflower*) on one of its beams. The beam's east end showed the letters 'ER HAR', which would be contained in the middle part of 'Mayflower Harwich'.

A short walk away through an orchard is the Friends' Meeting House, built in 1688, near which are the graves of the great Quaker, William Penn, founder and first governor of Pennsylvania, with his wives, Gulielma and Hannah, and 10 of their 16 children.

The presence of the Penn family graves, and the fact that Quakerism's founder, George Fox, worshipped here, have helped to make the Meeting House a focus of Quakerism worldwide. The interior of the house remains much as it was 300 years ago.

Places of Interest in the Neighbourhood
It's a Small World (Beaconsfield)
Rector v. Farmers (Beaconsfield)
Men of Iron (Gerrards Cross)

Sefton enjoys retirement at the Home of Rest for Horses.

47 Out of Harness

Position: Speen is 3 miles SE of Princes Risborough.
O.S. Map: Aylesbury area; Sheet 165; 1/50,000.
Map Ref: SU 835/993.
Access: From Slad Lane, SW of Speen village.

Judging by their eagerness for titbits, inmates of the immaculately kept Home of Rest for Horses much enjoy their daily visits from the public (though apples are not allowed).

The Home's most famous resident is the veteran Sefton, victim of the Hyde Park bombing in 1982. Thanks to the surgery and skilled care of the Royal Veterinary College, Sefton recovered from his appalling injuries. His duty done, he now holds court at Speen among a host of admirers. Echo, a police horse on duty at the bombing – but uninjured – is there too.

About 200 horses, ponies and donkeys stay at the stables in any one year, mostly for retirement, but some go to convalesce or a spell of rest from work. Others may stay while owners recover from illness, or while they cannot be cared for at home for financial or other reasons. There is always a long waiting list of people wanting to retire their horses.

The Home, which depends on voluntary donations, gifts and legacies, was founded in 1886 by Miss Ann Lindo – a friend of Anna Sewell, author of *Black Beauty* – who wanted working horses to have a better chance of survival. The Home is open every afternoon, 2pm-4pm (Tel: 0494 488464).

Places of Interest in the Neighbourhood
Disraeli's Admirer (High Wycombe)
Poet's Pleasure (Loosley Row)
The Pilot Who Saved a Town (Princes Risborough)

48 Silence in Court

Position: Long Crendon is a mile N of Thame.
O.S. Map: Aylesbury area; Sheet 165; 1/50,000.
Map Ref: SP 698/091.
Access: The Courthouse (NT) is in the High Street, near the churchyard.

The Courthouse is a gem of a building, guaranteed to waft the visitor back 500 years in a trice – it was built in the 1300s or 1400s. Set near the church in what is a delightful village in its own right, it has timber framing, red brick, wattle and daub. The atmosphere is helped along by the array of antique chairs and tables, and the white-painted oil-lamps.

Manorial courts were held in the upper room as far back as Henry V's time and until the 18th century. The ground floor housed the village poor until the early 1830s, when they transferred to the workhouse in nearby Thame. The building fell into decay in the 1890s. The lords of the manor intended to demolish it, but thanks to the vicar, who emphasised its value for church activities and as a store, the building was reprieved.

In 1900 the National Trust bought it from the three owners of the manors for £400, and raised a further £350 for restoration. Open April-end of September (Tel: 0296 84919).

Places of Interest in the Neighbourhood
Civil War Stronghold (Boarstall)
Gone to the Walls (Haddenham)
The Robbers' Hideout (Oakley)

Long Crendon's courthouse, dating back 500 years.

49 Poet's Pleasure

Position: A mile and a half SE of Princes Risborough.
O.S. Map: Aylesbury area; Sheet 165; 1/50,000.
Map Ref: SP 827/018.
Access: The Pink and Lily public house is at the junction of Pink Road and Pink Hill, a mile NE of Loosley Row.

The Pink and Lily inn was a favourite stop for the poet Rupert Brooke, who before the First World War (he died in 1915) would travel by train out from his home at Grantchester, Cambridge, to Wendover, and tramp the Chilterns.

The licensee, Clive Mason, believes that the other of 'two such men' in the following light-hearted poem, written by Brooke, could have been Winston Churchill.

> Never came there to the Pink
> Two such men as we, I think
> Never came there to the Lily
> Two men quite so richly silly...
> Were ever two so fierce and strong
> Who drank so deep and laughed so long,
> So proudly meek, so humbly proud,
> Who walked so far and sung so loud.

How the Pink and Lily acquired its name is also interesting. Tradition has it that a Mr Pink, head butler at Hampden House (Great Hampden, a mile or two east), and Miss Lily, a chambermaid, ran the inn together. Although never united in marriage, they were joined in the name of the inn.

Places of Interest in the Neighbourhood
A Rare Dovecote (Horsenden)
The Pilot Who Saved a Town (Princes Risborough)
Out of Harness (Speen)

50 Liberty's Ship

Position: The Lee village, three miles SW of Wendover.
O.S. Map: Aylesbury area; Sheet 165; 1/50,000.
Map Ref: SP 900/043.
Access: Pipers is in The Lee village, off the A413, near Wendover. The figurehead is visible from outside the gate.

Mrs Stewart-Liberty, a member of the Liberty family which founded the famous store in Regent Street, remembers the company's earlier days with a unique relic. Outside her house, Pipers, in The Lee, stands one of the fine old figureheads that once adorned the prows of the wooden ships of the 18th and 19th centuries. The timbers of the *Howe,* the last three-decker wooden warship to be built (launched in 1860, and never fired a shot in anger) were bought by the Libertys in the 1920s, by

The ancient ship's figurehead in a garden at The Lee.

which time the ship had become a training hulk on the Thames. The timbers were used in the rebuilding of Liberty's Regent Street store.

The figure on display is that of the much respected Admiral Earl (Richard) Howe, who became First Lord of the Admiralty in 1783. In 1794 he smashed the French Navy on what became known as The Glorious First of June.

Places of Interest in the Neighbourhood
Martyrs' Memorial (Amersham)
Puddingstone Church (Chesham)
Chilterns High Spot (Wendover)

Marlow's handsome suspension bridge across the Thames.

51 A Link with Hungary

Position: Marlow, on the Thames in South Bucks.
O.S. Map: Reading & Windsor area; Sheet 175; 1/50,000.
Map Ref: SU 852/862.
Access: The bridge leads the High Street over the Thames.

With its twin towers and the sweeping curves of its white-painted cables, this suspension bridge, with a span of 225 feet, is one of the most elegant pieces of architecture in the county.

It was built by William Clark in 1834, and in the light of public reaction to it he was asked to build one on similar lines in Budapest (connecting Buda and Pest across the Danube) and another at Hammersmith.

Places of Interest in the Neighbourhood
Twinge of Gout (Marlow)
Frankenstein's Birthplace (Marlow)
The Ferry Case (Medmenham)

52 Twinge of Gout

Position: Marlow, on the Thames in South Bucks.
O.S. Map: Reading & Windsor area; Sheet 175; 1/50,000.
Map Ref: SU 849/867.
Access: The 'gout road' obelisk stands in front of the Crown Hotel.

At the opposite end of the High Street from the suspension bridge is a slightly older and much less impressive structure: a large obelisk serving as a milestone.

  A clue to its origins is suggested by the places named: for example, Wycombe 5 miles, Aylesbury 22, Oxford-by-Stokenchurch 25, and Hatfield 36. Why Hatfield, a tiny village in Hertfordshire? Because the obelisk was erected in 1822 by the Reading and Hatfield Turnpike Trust, which improved the road via Henley, thus providing a shorter journey for the Cecils of Hatfield to the spa at Bath. Hence its nickname, 'gout road'. It leaves Marlow via West Street.

Places of Interest in the Neighbourhood
A Link with Hungary (Marlow)
Frankenstein's Birthplace (Marlow)
The Ferry Case (Medmenham)

The milestone along the 'gout road' at Marlow.

53 Frankenstein's Birthplace

Position: Marlow, on the Thames in South Bucks.
O.S. Map: Reading & Windsor area; Sheet 175; 1/50,000.
Map Ref: SU 846/864.
Access: Shelley cottages are in West Street. No access inside.

The four neat white-painted cottages in West Street, just east of the Sir
William Borlase School, formerly comprised Albion House, where
Percy and Mary Shelley lived in 1817. It was here that Mary completed
her story of Frankenstein, the scientist dabbler in magic and mystery
who discovered the secret of life. In his laboratory Frankenstein
assembled a man eight feet high – a monster that became a terror to its
creator.

How did Mary come to write such a story? It emerged in a light-
hearted way in the summer of 1816, when she, Byron and Shelley were
living on the banks of Lake Geneva. The Shelleys often spent their

Where the Shelleys lived at Marlow in 1817.

evenings with Byron at his house at Diodati. One wet week they amused themselves by reading German ghost stories, and they decided, as a way of passing the time, to write stories imitating them.

Mary's Frankenstein was judged to be the best. It was published the following year, and much praised. She died in 1851, having written a number of books in the meantime, but none has enjoyed such enduring popularity as Frankenstein.

Places of Interest in the Neighbourhood
A Link with Hungary (Marlow)
Twinge of Gout (Marlow)
The Ferry Case (Medmenham)

The plaque recalling the Ferry case in 1898.

54 The Ferry Case

Position: Medmenham, 3 miles W of Marlow.
O.S. Map: Reading & Windsor area; Sheet 175; 1/50,000.
Map Ref: SU 805/837.
Access: The commemorative ferry tablet is on the right beyond a wooden bridge at the southern end of Ferry Lane.

Medmenham provided the background for a series of court actions in 1898, whose outcome is now commemorated by a plaque. In one case, Robert Hudson claimed an injunction to restrain John Weyman from trespassing on his land at Medmenham Ferry and carting bricks across what Weyman stated was a public highway.

The second action was brought against Robert Hudson to restrain him from obstructing and encroaching on the highway; and from failing to keep open the public ferry.

The judge ruled that the ferry and the public highway to it on each side of the river were public, and should be maintained as such.

The ruined abbey, scene of orgies associated with the Hell Fire Club (see No 78, 'Hell Fire Days'), is incorporated into the house visible a hundred yards or so along the river to the left.

Places of Interest in the Neighbourhood
A Link with Hungary (Marlow)
Twinge of Gout (Marlow)
Frankenstein's Birthplace (Marlow)

55 Paxton's Finest

Position: Approach Mentmore Towers from Mentmore village, two miles SE of Wing.
O.S. Map: Aylesbury area; Sheet 165; 1/50,000.
Map Ref: SP 902/197.
Access: Through the gates and up the drive from Mentmore village.

Sir Joseph Paxton is best-known for building the Crystal Palace, venue of that impressive shop-window of Victorian England, the Great Exhibition of 1851. Sadly, the Crystal Palace burned down in 1936, leaving this as Paxton's finest and most imposing surviving work, built in 1852, the year following the Great Exhibition.

Unlike the Crystal Palace, Mentmore Towers, which Paxton also designed, is more solidly built in Ancaster stone; though the Paxton touch is revealed in the glass roof of the Grand Hall.

Mentmore Towers was originally built for Baron Meyer de Rothschild, and was later owned by the Earls of Rosebery. Visitors can see the house and grounds on Sundays and Bank Holidays, thanks to the present owners, the Maharishi University of Natural Law, whose headquarters it has become.

Places of Interest in the Neighbourhood
Scene of the Crime (Cheddington)
In Case of Fire (Ivinghoe)
Down on the Ancient Farm (Pitstone)

56 A City Clad in Green

Position: Milton Keynes is about 8 miles NE of Buckingham.
O.S. Map: Northampton & Milton Keynes area; Sheet 152; 1/50,000.
Map Ref: SP 855/391.
Access: Queens Court is in Central Milton Keynes, bounded by Saxon
Gate, Midsummer Boulevard, Silbury Boulevard and Secklow Gate.

'Vox Pop', a sculpture by John Clinch, has been a prominent feature of
Queens Court in the shopping complex of central Milton Keynes since
1988. It offsets with a human touch the austere straight lines of the
centre of the city, though there is no shortage of humanity when the
shops are open.

  This is just one of dozens of works of art scattered throughout Milton
Keynes, and which are carefully mapped in the city's publicity. The city
requires a great deal of getting used to: it is not easy to find one's way

Vox Pop: a sculpture in Milton Keynes city centre.

round because of the uniformity of the road layout, constructed on the Roman grid system.

Milton Keynes was designated in 1967 to have an ultimate population of more than 200,000 – overspill from London. It possesses great beauty of an innovatory kind, having absorbed into its conurbation four existing towns – Bletchley, Stony Stratford, Wolverton and New Bradwell. But, as the corporation asserts, Milton Keynes has not replaced the countryside, but rather grown into it.

The city's landscaping is brilliantly conceived: it claims to be the greenest city in the country. More than 14 million trees and shrubs were planted over 20 years, and more than a sixth of the city consists of parkland. It is, in fact, an industrial city, though you would hardly know it.

Places of Interest in the Neighbourhood
Solving the Enigma (Bletchley)
Allotted Span (Newport Pagnell)
Tall Stories (Stony Stratford)

57 Allotted Span

Position: Tickford is on the edge of Newport Pagnell.
O.S. Map: Northampton & Milton Keynes area; Sheet 152; 1/50,000.
Map Ref: SP 878/439.
Access: Tickford Bridge takes the B256 across the Ouse. Approach
along the A509.

The old iron bridge bestriding the Ouse (or Lovat) at Tickford is a relic
of the Industrial Revolution. Tickford's bridge is unique in Britain,
being the earliest iron bridge still in daily use by road traffic. It dates
back to 1810, the year inscribed on it. The first such bridge in the world
was built at Coalbrookdale, Shropshire, by Abraham Darby in 1779,
but although it still survives it is used only by pedestrians.

Places of Interest in the Neighbourhood
Solving the Enigma (Bletchley)
A City Clad in Green (Milton Keynes)
Tall Stories (Stony Stratford)

The Industrial Revolution bridge at Newport Pagnell.

58 Honour for a Horse

Position: Latimer, E of Chesham, on the Herts border.
O.S. Map: Luton, Hertford area; Sheet 166; 1/50,000.
Map Ref: TQ 003/993.
Access: The monument is under a tree on the village green.

Men, not animals, are usually honoured in war. In Latimer village, though, both are noticed. Alongside the memorial to soldiers who fell in the Boer War is a stone mound on the Green bearing plaques to a horse. One inscription reads: 'The horse ridden by General de Villebois Mareuil at the Battle of Boshof, S. Africa, 5th April 1900, in which the General was killed and the horse wounded'.

A second inscription notes that the horse, Villebois, was brought to England by Major General Lord Chesham later that year. It died in 1911.

Places of Interest in the Neighbourhood
Paradise Conserved (Chalfont St Giles)
Buildings on the Move (Chalfont St Giles)
An Unfaithful Queen (Chenies)

Warhorse memorial under a tree at Latimer.

59 Miracle Man

Position: North Marston is 4 miles NW of Aylesbury.
O.S. Map: Aylesbury area; Sheet 165; 1/50,000.
Map Ref: SP 777/227.
Access: From Church Street.

North Marston's rector, John Schorne, had a reputation as a miracle worker in the Middle Ages, and at one time the church contained a shrine to him. Schorne was rector there from 1290 until he died in 1314. Before that he held the living at Monks Risborough.

What had brought him these wonderful powers was his blessing of a local hillside spring, which served as one of the village's main sources of water. The water was said to be a curative for gout, rheumatism and disorders of the eye.

However, it was not so much the cures that earned Schorne a minor place in history and folklore, but his achievement in magicking the devil into a boot (a feat which gave rise to Jack-in-the-Box toys). He was revered – though not officially – as a saint, and indeed after his death he had a statue in a shrine at the eastern end of the south aisle of the parish church, and in London, pilgrims' badges bore his picture and the boot.

Matters apparently got out of hand when crowds of pilgrims overwhelmed the shrine, and as the result of a petition to the Pope, both shrine and relics were transferred to St George's Chapel, Windsor in 1481.

Places of Interest in the Neighbourhood
Unknown Warriors (Hardwick)
Tribute to Florence (Middle Claydon)
Birthplace of Mrs Miniver (Whitchurch)

60 The Robbers' Hideout

Position: Leatherslade Farm is about a mile E of Oakley.
O.S. Map: Aylesbury area; Sheet 165; 1/50,000.
Map Ref: SP 654/124.
Access: Visible from B4011.

The village of Oakley and Leatherslade Farm, on the outskirts of the village, were thrust into the limelight of notoriety in August 1963. Mysterious visitors appeared in the village – seldom seen and only then when buying provisions at the local store.

When the news broke of the Great Train Robbery at Cheddington, the truth emerged: the robbers had lain low for three months at Leatherslade before the robbery. And back to Leatherslade they went afterwards with their mailbags stuffed with notes.

No-one suspected anything amiss, as the farm was on a hillside and at the end of a lonely track. (See No 22, 'Scene of the Crime'.)

Places of Interest in the Neighbourhood
Out for the Ducks (Boarstall)
Gone to the Walls (Haddenham)
Silence in Court (Long Crendon)

61 Hymns and Pancakes

Position: Olney is 4 miles N of Newport Pagnell.
O.S. Map: Northampton & Milton Keynes area; Sheet 152; 1/50,000.
Map Ref: SP 890/512.
Access: The village stands on the A509.

Formerly one of the county's lace-making towns, Olney is better-known for hymns and pancakes. Pancakes, traditional feature of Shrove Tuesday, originated when housewives had to use up dairy products and eggs – which in the Middle Ages were forbidden foods in Lent.

In 1445, in Olney, the Pancake Race became a regular feature of Shrove Tuesdays. A bell-clanging by the town crier starts the race, run over 415 yards from the Market Place to the church. During the run, each competitor must toss and catch her pancake three times. The winner gets a prayer book and a kiss from the sexton.

In Orchard Side, at the bottom of Market Place, between 1768 and 1786, the poet William Cowper worked on his famous poems, including

Housewives make a dash for it in Olney's pancake race.

'The Task' (see No 80, 'Cowper's Retreat') and 'John Gilpin'. He also wrote 'Olney Hymns' with John Newton, a slaveship captain converted to Christianity, who was a curate in Olney and later Rector of St Mary Woolnoth, in the City of London.

From Newton's pen came 260 hymns, including 'Amazing Grace', 'How sweet the name of Jesus sounds' and 'Glorious things of Thee are spoken'. Cowper wrote 67, including 'God moves in a mysterious way', 'Jesus where'er Thy people meet', and 'Hark my soul! It is the Lord'.

Orchard Side, now a museum, contains many possessions of Cowper and Newton, including the poet's greatcoat and waistcoat.

Cowper died in 1800, and is buried at East Dereham, Norfolk. Newton's body, originally at St Mary Woolnoth, was brought back to Olney, where he is buried in the left-hand corner of the churchyard.

Places of Interest in the Neighbourhood
A City Clad in Green (Milton Keynes)
Allotted Span (Newport Pagnell)
Tall Stories (Stony Stratford)

The entrance to Pinewood Studios, where top British films were made.

62 Carry On Filming

Position: Pinewood Studios are just SE of Fulmer.
O.S. Map: West London area; Sheet 176; 1/50,000.
Map Ref: SU 017/844.
Access: A mile N of junction A412 and A4007.

From behind the mock-medieval facade of Pinewood Studios' half-timbered entrance lodge have emerged some of the cinema's favourite films. The heyday of the British film industry may be over, but production goes on.

When the studios opened in 1936, the first films made there were 'London Melody' (which began life at Elstree), starring Anna Neagle and Tillio Carminatti, and Carol Reed's 'Talk of the Devil'.

At that time British films were competing directly with better-resourced Hollywood; all too often they finished up as second features. During the Second World War the studios were requisitioned for emergency food supplies.

After the war, they reopened with great optimism, guided by the financial genius J. Arthur Rank. Two classic British films made there in 1947 were 'The Red Shoes', starring Moira Shearer, and 'Oliver Twist' (Alec Guinness as Fagin), made by David Lean following his 'Great Expectations' the previous year.

One of Pinewood's biggest successes was 'Genevieve', starring Kay Kendall and Kenneth More. Others were the Titanic disaster film 'A Night to Remember', 'The Angry Silence', Bryan Forbes's 'Whistle Down the Wind', 'Those Magnificent Men in Their Flying Machines' and 'The Battle of Britain'.

Among Pinewood's consistent winners have been the James Bond films – which set the pace for a host of other secret agent thrillers – and the 'Carry On' films, of which at least 28 have been made there.

Places of Interest in the Neighbourhood
Death of 'His Majesty' (Burnham Beeches)
Men of Iron (Gerrards Cross)
Remembering the Elegy (Stoke Poges)

63 Down on the Ancient Farm

Position: Pitstone is about 6 miles SW of Dunstable.
O.S. Map: Aylesbury area; Sheet 165; 1/50,000.
Map Ref: SP 937/156.
Access: Pitstone Green Farm Museum is near the roundabout at the junction of Vicarage Road and Marsworth Road (B489).

This farm has been in the family of the present owner, Jeff Hawkins, who was born here, since 1808. For many years the Pitstone Local History Society has put on show a remarkable collection of farm machinery and bygones, some dating back to the 1800s. Exhibits include implements used in lacemaking – one of Buckinghamshire's traditional industries – and straw-plaiting (for the Luton hat industry).

Others are drawn from Mr Hawkins's own collection: his childhood hoop, made by the local blacksmith, is there, along with a road wagon which took him and other children on Sunday School outings; and photographs of his family working on the farm.

One room shows what a typical farmhouse kitchen was like in former days, with all the old implements – butter-maker, kitchen range, dresser and china. Other bygones include birthday cards, Victorian clothes and toys.

There are several shops containing craftsmen's tools – a carpenter's, cobbler's, plumber's and brushmaker's. On special days the forge is in action, with a smith demonstrating his craft.

Pitstone Green Farm Museum (Tel: 0296 668223) is normally open on the last Sunday in the month between May and September, interspersed with three activity open days. Parties at other times by appointment.

Places of Interest in the Neighbourhood
Point of View (Ivinghoe)
In Case of Fire (Ivinghoe)
Old Mill by the Stream (Ivinghoe)

64 Old Mill by the Stream

Position: The watermill is at Ford End Farm, 600 yards from Ivinghoe
church down Station Road (the B488 to Leighton Buzzard).
O.S. Map: Aylesbury area; Sheet 165; 1/50,000.
Map Ref: SP 941/166.
Access: From Station Road, through farmyard.

There are records that this old watermill was working in the late 1700s,
though the Pitstone Local History Society, which has lovingly restored
it, believes its origins are much earlier. The Victoria County History
notes that a watermill in Ivinghoe was owned in the 14th century by two

The ancient Ford End Farm watermill at Ivinghoe.

families, but whether this was the mill referred to is uncertain. The initials and date, 'W. H. 1795' on a wall seem to confirm the mill's occupation by a William Heley, who was recorded in 1798 as grinding 16 sacks of grain a week.

The mill-wheel is of the overshot type, with metal buckets and cast-iron rim, and is driven by a head of water from the mill pond – originally a moat round the first farmhouse – in turn filled by water from springs in the chalk about half a mile away.

One interesting feature of the mill is the pool, downstream from the wheel, which was used for washing sheep. They were brought from local farms for washing before they were shorn because clean wool sold at a better price than unwashed wool.

The mill was in use until 1963, and has been restored to working order. Flour-milling demonstrations are usually given in the afternoons of the second Sundays in June, July and September, and on the Bank Holiday Mondays in May and August. Inquiries 0582 600391; party bookings 0296 668152.

Places of Interest in the Neighbourhood
Point of View (Ivinghoe)
In Case of Fire (Ivinghoe)
Down on the Ancient Farm (Pitstone)

Obelisk in honour of local hero John Hampden.

65 In Memory of Hampden

Position: Prestwood is 4 miles SE of Princes Risborough.
O.S. Map: Aylesbury area; Sheet 165; 1/50,000.
Map Ref: SP 863/019.
Access: Take Honor End Lane from Prestwood. Hampden monument is just beyond Honor End Farm through small gate on right.

This obelisk, in memory of John Hampden, the local hero who defied Charles I, is almost hidden in a small hedged enclosure, and is easily missed. The inscription, which is barely legible, notes: 'For these lands in Stoke Mandeville, John Hampden was assessed in twenty shillings Ship Money levied by command of the king without authority of law.' (See also No 5, 'When Hampden said 'No'.)

John Hampden lived at Hampden House, which still stands, a mile away in Great Hampden (map ref SP 848/025). He is buried in the church opposite. The house, now occupied by a commercial company, is regrettably never open to the public, but the church is open on Sundays.

Places of Interest in the Neighbourhood
When Hampden Said No (Aylesbury)
Out of Harness (Speen)
The Pilot Who Saved a Town (Princes Risborough)

66 The Pilot Who Saved a Town

Position: Princes Risborough is 4 miles S of Aylesbury.
O.S. Map: Aylesbury area; Sheet 165; 1/50,000.
Map Ref: SP 808/033.
Access: The memorial is in front of Princes Risborough library, at the junction of High Street and Bell Street.

A memorial plaque and tree seat outside Princes Risborough Public Library, placed there in 1992, commemorate a brave American pilot, Lt Clyde W. Cosper, whose act of heroism and self-sacrifice saved the town from great loss of life.

Clyde W. Cosper

The memorial to a brave airman at Princes Risborough.

In 1943, a Flying Fortress of the US Air Force, flown by Cosper, took off from Thurleigh airfield, Bedfordshire, to join a raid on German U-boat pens at Bremen. In a storm over Princes Risborough, his plane began to break up and fly out of control. Cosper immediately ordered the crew of nine to bale out. With the plane clearly doomed, he remained with the plane and guided it away from the town, crashlanding it in a field near Summerleys Road. For his bravery and presence of mind Cosper was awarded three US decorations posthumously: the Silver Star, the Air Medal and the Purple Heart.

In the Booker Aircraft Museum (see No 13, 'Relics of the Air Wars') are the officer's identification tag, cap badge, some of the Fortress's instruments, and his aircraft's propeller blade. Lt Cosper is buried in his home state of Texas.

Places of Interest in the Neighbourhood
A Rare Dovecote (Princes Risborough)
Crosses in Chalk (Princes Risborough)
Chilterns High Spot (Wendover)

67 Crosses in Chalk

Position: Whiteleaf Cross is half a mile NE of Princes Risborough;
Bledlow Cross is on Wain Hill, a mile or so E of Chinnor, which is three
miles SW of Princes Risborough.
O.S. Map: Aylesbury & Leighton Buzzard area; Sheet 165; 1/50,000.
Map Refs: Whiteleaf, SP 823/039; Bledlow, SP 768/009.
Access: Whiteleaf: Up Peters Lane, park in Whiteleaf Hill car park,
then walk along footpath. Bledlow: Turn off Chinnor Road into Hill
Top Lane, then walk.

The origins of both these crosses, cut in chalk on hillsides four miles
apart, is unknown, but neither is thought to be earlier than the 17th
century. Whiteleaf is on a two-acre site and is 80ft long and 72 feet
wide, with a large pyramid-shaped base. Bledlow's cross is slightly
smaller and without a base.

   The crosses are elusive if sought from a distance, but Whiteleaf can be
glimpsed from the A4010 near Princes Risborough.

Places of Interest in the Neighbourhood
A Rare Dovecote (Princes Risborough)
The Pilot Who Saved a Town (Princes Risborough)
Chilterns High Spot (Wendover)

The two mysterious crosses on hillsides at Whiteleaf and Bledlow.

68 Getting Steamed Up

Position: Quainton is 4 miles NW of Aylesbury.
O.S. Map: Aylesbury area; Sheet 165; 1/50,000.
Map Ref: SP 737/190.
Access: Turn off the A41(T) at Waddesdon. Quainton Road station
is a mile or so N towards Quainton village.

Buckinghamshire Railway Centre contains a real country railway
station, once a BR station but now a lively focus for enthusiasts and
members of a public eager for a nostalgic whiff of smoke and steam.
There are automatic machines, hanging baskets of flowers, ticket office,
waiting room, platforms, footbridge, semaphore signals, signal-box,
refreshment coach and cloakrooms.
   The centre possesses many main-line and individual steam and diesel

Buckinghamshire Railway Centre, Quainton.

locos. Steam trains chug up and down the stretch of line on special open days during the year, but locomotives such as the spick-and-span maroon-liveried Metropolitan 1 regularly take passengers for a spin on normal visiting days.

The Quainton Railway Society, which owns and operates the Buckinghamshire Railway Centre, has a continous programme of restoring old locomotives and rolling stock, and possesses many antique wagons such as the freight trucks and brake vans to be seen in the sidings – not forgetting a London Underground train. Over 16 years, the Society restored the fine Great Western Railway locomotive King Edward I, built in 1920 and bought from the scrapyard in 1962. One of the Society's most important restorations is a locomotive from South Africa, which will be the biggest working steam loco in Britain.

A particular source of pride is a London and North Western Railway dining car, built in 1901 and used for 15 years between Euston and north-west England before becoming part of the royal train. The diner is now used for special functions, such as Victorian teas, and is included in the trains once a month in the summer. Open Easter to end of October (Tel: 029 675 450).

Places of Interest in the Neighbourhood
Unknown Warriors (Hardwick)
Tribute to Florence (Middle Claydon)
Mrs Miniver's Birthplace (Whitchurch)

69 Elizabeth I Dined Here

Position: Quarrendon village ruin is half a mile NW of Aylesbury.
O.S. Map: Aylesbury area; Sheet 165; 1/50,000.
Map Ref: SP 802/158.
Access: A few yards north of the Thame bridge, on Bicester Road, A41
(T) take footpath opposite layby on left and walk through two fields.
Ruin and moat are to the right, across the river Thame.

There's not much left to see of old Quarrendon. Only the ruin of the late
13th-century church of St Peter reminds the walker that a village once
stood here. St Peter's has been in this sad condition for years; even in
1817 *The Gentleman's Magazine* referred to it as 'a melancholy object of
contemplation'.

Sir Henry Lee, ancestor of General Lee, leader of the south in the
American Civil War, entertained Queen Elizabeth I in the family's
grand mansion here in 1592, but nothing is left of the house.

Sir Henry's monument was once in the church here; that of his wife is
in St Mary's Church, Aylesbury (see No 7, 'Evergreen Response').

Places of Interest in the Neighbourhood
When Hampden Said No (Aylesbury)
Cromwell Sat Here (Aylesbury)
Evergreen Response (Aylesbury)

70 The Gentle Giants

Position: The Shire Horse Centre is in Chalfont St Giles, 2 miles SW of Amersham.
O.S. Map: West London area; Sheet 176; 1/50,000.
Map Ref: SU 012/933.
Access: Model Farm is half a mile along Gorelands Lane, near junction with Brallings Lane.

It's many a year since Shire horses were seen on regular duty in London's streets, hauling drays of beer from the brewers to the public houses. But Shires are not being allowed to die out – not while there are still brewers, and men such as Derek Croft, a drayman in the 1950s, to breed them and foster public interest in them. Croft's first job when he left school was working with Shires. Now, at his Chalfont Shire Centre, he has nearly 50 of them, which he uses for showing and demonstrations.

Shires are as sturdy as they look. They live until their mid-20s, though one has survived till he was 31. One of the most popular is Major, foaled in 1974, who takes part in ploughing and showing competitions.

The Centre has what is claimed to be the biggest collection of harness in Britain – masses of shining leather and shimmering brass – and some prize horse-drawn vehicles. Among the latter are two London horse-buses, dated 1870 and 1894 – still carrying their destination names – and a brewer's dray, railway coal cart, old-fashioned gypsy caravan and farm carts. The Centre is open between March and October (Tel: 0494 872304).

Places of Interest in the Neighbourhood
From Coaching Days (Chalfont Common)
Buildings on the Move (Chalfont St Giles)
Paradise Conserved (Chalfont St Giles)

71 Norman Glory

Position: Stewkley is 4 miles S of Milton Keynes.
O.S. Map: Aylesbury area; Sheet 165; 1/50,000.
Map Ref: SP 852/261.
Access: The parish church is alongside B4032.

The Normans built about 6,000 churches in Britain, and St Michael &
All Angels Church in Stewkley is one of very few that are 'pure' –
unadorned by later additions. Pevsner, giving its probable date as
1140-50, describes all parts as being 'sumptuously decorated'. It is built
of limestone rubble mixed with local iron limestone. A close look at the
highly decorative Norman detail is rewarding. There is plenty of the
characteristic zigzagging, especially in the magnificent west front, which
also features dragons under the arch.

  Stewkley is one of the longest villages in England – about two miles
– and the church is halfway along it. This 800-year-old survivor was
threatened not many years ago by the possibility of a third London
airport in the area. Its presence, and architectural importance, were
vital factors that helped ward off the danger. A providential rescue, one
might say.

Places of Interest in the Neighbourhood
Solving the Enigma (Bletchley)
A City Clad in Green (Milton Keynes)
Allotted Span (Newport Pagnell)

The exquisite Norman doorway at Stewkley church.

72 Remembering the Elegy

Position: Stoke Poges, near the county border, just N of Slough.
O.S. Map: Reading & Windsor area; Sheet 175; 1/50,000.
Map Ref: SU 975/828.
Access: From B146, turn into Church Lane, then along path to church.

Thomas Gray wrote several fine poems, but the one that made him famous was the 'Elegy Written in a Country Churchyard', beginning 'The curfew tolls the knell of parting day...'. Gray is buried in the churchyard of St Giles's in Stoke Poges – the very churchyard where the Elegy is thought to have been written. His tomb, a slab of stone on brick, is also that of his beloved aunt and mother, and can be seen outside the east end of the church.

The inscription written by Gray about his mother, reads: 'Dorothy Gray, widow, the careful, tender mother of many children, one of whom alone had the misfortune to survive her'. Gray was of course that survivor and was buried with her at his own wish.

One would have thought this modest churchyard memorial enough for Gray, but a stroll through a patch of National Trust-owned woodland named after him, takes the visitor to an 18th-century monument – a 20ft high sarcophagus, mounted on a plinth and inscribed with verses from the Elegy. The monument was designed by James Wyatt and erected in 1799 by Jack Penn, grandson of William Penn.

Places of Interest in the Neighbourhood
It's a Small World (Beaconsfield)
Death of 'His Majesty' (Burnham Beeches)
Men of Iron (Gerrards Cross)

The memorial to Thomas Gray at Stoke Poges.

73 Tall Stories

Position: Stony Stratford is on the W extremity of Milton Keynes.
O.S. Map: Northampton & Milton Keynes area; Sheet 152; 1/50,000.
Map Ref: SP 786/406.
Access: The two inns are near each other at the junction of London
Road and Church Street.

The phrase 'cock and bull story', meaning a tale that is highly suspect, is
said to have been derived from the names of two neighbouring public
houses, the Cock and the Bull, in the main street at Stony Stratford.

   The two hostelries are referred to in Brewer's *Dictionary of Phrase and
Fable:* 'There is a story at Stony Stratford that in the coaching days the
London coach changed horses at the Bull and and the Birmingham
coach at the Cock. From the exchange of jests and stories between the
waiting passengers of both coaches the Cock and Bull story is said to
have originated.'

Places of Interest in the Neighbourhood
Solving the Enigma (Bletchley)
A City Clad in Green (Milton Keynes)
Hymns and Pancakes (Olney)

Signs of The Cock and The Bull inns at Stony Stratford.

74 The Biggest Garden of All

Position: Stowe is 2 miles NW of Buckingham.
O.S. Map: Northampton & Milton Keynes area; Sheet 152; 1/50,000.
Map Ref: SP 675/375.
Access: Stowe Landscape Gardens (NT) can be reached along a drive
from the A422 out of Buckingham.

The Temple of British Worthies is one of the most interesting of the
many monuments, columns, arches, artificial ruins and lakes which
adorn these beautiful gardens in the grounds of Stowe School. They
have been described as the largest work of art in Britain.

The Temple was designed by William Kent in 1733 – other monu-

The Temple of Worthies, a feature of Stowe Landscape Gardens.

ments were his work and that of James Gibbs – and pays tribute in the form of stone busts by Rysbrack and Scheemakers to leading figures in the country's history. These are strung out in an impressive curved gallery of niches on the east bank of the river Styx and include King Alfred, the Black Prince, Elizabeth I, William III, Raleigh, Drake, Shakespeare, Milton, Pope, Bacon, Locke, Newton, Inigo Jones, Thomas Gresham and John Hampden. And there is Sir John Barnard MP – worthy only for voting in support of Lord Cobham, owner of Stowe, against the Excise Bill!

Viscount Cobham was a member of the Temple family, which with its successor, the Grenvilles, owned and initiated the landscaping of Stowe's gardens in the 18th century. They were originally the work of Vanbrugh, but Kent and Gibbs began endowing a more natural look, a process continued by 'Capability' Brown, head gardener here for ten years.

The house was sold in 1921 and became the public school it is today, but the gardens themselves belong to the National Trust. Allow two hours to tour. Open in school holidays; limited openings during term (Tel: 0280 822850).

Places of Interest in the Neighbourhood
Strongpoint of the Law (Buckingham)
Chantry Chapel (Buckingham)
Tribute to Florence (Middle Claydon)

75 Keeper of the Queen's Swans

Position: The swan-uppers can be seen at work on the Thames during
the third week every July, along Buckinghamshire's southern border
between Dorney Reach in the E to Fawley Court in the W.
O.S. Map: Reading, Windsor area; Sheet 175, 1:50,000.
Map Refs: SU 915/790, Dorney Reach; SU 765/842, Fawley Court.

Every year, Captain John Turk spends five days on the Thames for
what sounds like a holiday. It is part of his duties as the Queen's Swan
Keeper, which also involves caring for the swans all the year round.
Captain Turk was appointed to the post in 1963.

Although every mute swan in Britain belongs to the Queen, Captain
Turk is concerned only with those on the Thames. The swan-upping
process starts at Sunbury-on-Thames, Middlesex, and works up the
river over five days with his crew past Marlow, in Buckinghamshire, to
Day's Lock in Oxfordshire, a distance of about 70 miles.

He and swan-upping crews from two City livery companies, the
Vintners and Dyers, with ancient rights to swans on the Thames, track
down all the newly-hatched broods. These are then distributed among
the three interested parties – the Queen, the Vintners' and the Dyers'
Companies – according to the ownership established by identifying
marks on the beaks of the parents. The Queen's cygnets have no mark,
but the two livery companies cut nicks in the soft tissue of a cygnet's
beak. The Vintners' have two nicks – one on each side of the beak – and
the Dyers', one nick on one side.

When they reach Windsor, and are within sight of the castle, the crews
pause to take part in a little ceremony. They 'toss' their oars (i.e. hold
them vertically), in salute to the Queen, and drink a loyal toast.

The ancient custom of swan-upping enables up to around 150 cygnets
to be found and identified every year.

76 Brunel's Feat – or Folly?

Position: Railway bridge connecting Taplow and Maidenhead.
O.S. Map: Reading & Windsor area; Sheet 175; 1/50,000.
Map Ref: SU 901/810.
Access: The bridge is along River Road.

In 1975 a commemorative plaque was placed on this bridge as part of the celebrations to mark European Architectural Heritage Year. The plaque was a tribute to its builder, the famous railway engineer Isambard Kingdom Brunel.

In order to avoid unnecessary interference with navigation, Brunel used only two spans. The bridge is unique because the two brick arches are the widest and flattest in the world – 128 feet, with a rise of only 24 feet. The plaque refers to the 'sounding arch', no doubt because of the echoes produced by the parabolic construction of the arches. A shout from the towpath reverberates for many seconds.

Brunel's building method was attacked as extravagant folly – it was said the shallow arches would soon collapse. Cracks did show in the brickwork of one arch when it was built, but the other held. The contractor then admitted he had eased the centering – the temporary supporting framework – in the cracked arch before the cement had set. Forecasts that it was not strong enough to bear a train quickly proved false.

J. M. W. Turner also made the bridge famous by using it as the setting for his famous picture 'Rain, Steam and Speed', which hangs in the National Gallery, and shows a broad-gauge locomotive crossing the bridge.

Places of Interest in the Neighbourhood
Death of 'His Majesty' (Burnham Beeches)
Riverside Grandeur (Cliveden)
Men of Iron (Gerrards Cross)

Brunel's unique railway bridge at Taplow.

77 A Taste of France

Position: Waddesdon Manor (NT) is 4 miles NW of Aylesbury.
O.S. Map: Aylesbury area; Sheet 165; 1/50,000.
Map Ref: SP 733/165.
Access: Along drive from Waddesdon village, A41(T).

Baron Ferdinand de Rothschild set his chateau, designed by Gabriel-Hippolyte Destailleur, on a hill, at a stroke converting a corner of England into a 'coin de France', aided by its curious cluster of pinnacles and domes, towers and turrets. Now a National Trust property, it was built between 1874 and 1889, and stands in formal gardens, with yews, fountain pool and statuary.

The manor's rooms are in French style, too, with 18th-century furniture, carpets and porcelain. Portraits by Gainsborough, Reynolds and Romney decorate the walls, with a permanent exhibition of women's dresses of the 1860s.

(The Manor is at present closed because of massive repair and restoration work, and is not expected to reopen before 1994. Gardens open March until Christmas. Tel: 0296 651211).

Places of Interest in the Neighbourhood
When Hampden Said No (Aylesbury)
Evergreen Response (Aylesbury)
All Steamed Up (Quainton)

78 Hell Fire Days

Position: West Wycombe Park (NT) is 3 miles W of High Wycombe.
O.S. Map: Reading, Windsor area; Sheet 175; 1/50,000.
Map Ref: SU 830/933.
Access: Through gate on western edge of West Wycombe village.

West Wycombe House, a Palladian-style mansion standing in grounds
landscaped by Capability Brown, has been the seat of the Dashwood
family since 1698. On the other side of the road from the main gate is
a path leading up the hill to the Georgian Church of St Lawrence,
surmounting whose tower is a huge hollow golden ball, visible for miles.
This, so the story goes, is where the notorious Hell Fire Club (motto:
'Do What You Will'), founded by Sir Francis Dashwood's ancestors,
occasionally held its meetings.

The golden ball surmounting the tower of the Church of St Lawrence.

The heart of Paul Whitehead, steward of the Club, was buried with ceremony in the Mausoleum on the hill, but in bizarre fashion. Until 1829, when the heart was stolen, it had been frequently taken out and shown to visitors. The urn that contained it is still there. Many of the more scandalous activities of the club, including its reputed orgies, took place at Medmenham, about seven miles south (map ref: SU 805/845) on the Thames, where Sir Francis had refashioned the ruins of the Cistercian abbey. These now form part of a private house (see No 54, 'The Ferry Case).

The present Sir Francis, 11th Baronet and present incumbent of West Wycombe House and Park, spent much time in the 1950s exploring the Caves – then wet, slippery and dangerous. One cleric claimed that an evil influence was at work there; Sir Francis himself admits to finding them 'rather creepy'.

Today the Caves are open to the public. Roughly S-shaped, they depict at intervals various scenes – including models of members of the Hell Fire Club. These included, during the club's life in the mid-1700s, politicians (at least 10 MPs, John Wilkes among them) as well as poets, dons and the painter William Hogarth. A visit to the house and grounds are a delightful antidote for any 'creepy' thoughts. Open April and May, grounds only; June-August, house and grounds (Tel: 0494 24411).

Places of Interest in the Neighbourhood
The 'UFO' of 1871 (Downley)
Sitting Pretty (High Wycombe)
In Praise of Women (High Wycombe)

79 A Little on the Wild Side

Position: Weston Underwood is about a mile SW of Olney, north of
Milton Keynes.
O.S. Map: Northampton & Milton Keynes area; Sheet 152; 1/50,000.
Map Ref: SP 868/512.
Access: The Flamingo Gardens and Zoo are reached from Weston
Underwood High Street.

A collection of around 40 flamingoes is a principal feature of the
Flamingo Gardens and Zoological Park in Weston Underwood – the
only zoo in the county.

Christopher Marler opened the zoo in 1961, and has since had great
success in breeding many interesting creatures in as natural surround-

Feeding time for flamingoes at Weston Underwood.

ings as possible. All told, there are around 800 inmates spread over 160 species.

Among the animals that roam – and breed – in its 15 acres are white wallabies, American bison, red buffalo, antelopes and llamas. There are also an unusual species of wild sheep called moufflon – natives of the mountainous regions of southern Europe.

The characteristic salmon-pink hues of the Caribbean flamingoes' plumage is a result of ingesting carotene, which is a natural constituent of their diet. In captivity a shrimp mix introduces the required carotene into their food.

The zoo's birds, many of them rare, form a dazzlingly colourful collection. Peafowl, cranes, cockatoos, eagles (one of them, the bald-headed eagle, is the symbol of the United States), toucans, storks, vultures and pelicans. In the arboretum known as The Wilderness, which forms part of the zoo area, are several memorials – some to dogs – bearing words by the poet Cowper, friend of his patrons, the local Throckmorton family, who then owned the land. Open Easter to end of September (Tel: 0234 711451).

Places of Interest in the Neighbourhood
A City Clad in Green (Milton Keynes)
Allotted Span (Newport Pagnell)
Hymns and Pancakes (Olney)

80 Cowper's Retreat

Position: Weston Underwood is a mile SW of Olney, N of Milton
Keynes.
O.S. Map: Northampton & Milton Keynes area; Sheet 152; 1/50,000.
Map Ref: SP 862/513.
Access: Cowper's Alcove is along Wood Lane from the High Street.

The poet William Cowper (see No 61, 'Hymns and Pancakes') spent his
last happy years in this village – which he described as the loveliest
in England – in the two-storey house with seven prominent dormer
windows that can be seen in the single main street. He lived in Olney
and Weston Underwood from 1783 to 1795. Cowper was a friend of the
local Throckmorton family, who greatly encouraged him, and he wrote
verses for their memorials, now in the grounds of the Flamingo Park
and Zoo (see No 79, 'A Little on the Wild Side').

A hundred yards or so from the inn named after him, the Cowper's

Many of William Cowper's later works were written in The Alcove.

Oak, is Wood Lane, and half a mile up the hill and round to the right is Cowper's Alcove (erected by the Throckmortons in 1753), where the poet would sit and draw inspiration from the splendid view round to Olney church. Many of his last works are thought to have been written here. A plaque in the Alcove contains lines from his poem, 'The Task': 'The summit gained, behold the proud alcove that crowned it . . .'

The stone gateway spanning Weston Underwood High Street makes an imposing entrance to the village; it is practically all that is left of the manor that once belonged to the Throckmortons.

Places of Interest in the Neighbourhood
A City Clad in Green (Milton Keynes)
Hymns and Pancakes (Olney)
A Little on the Wild Side (Weston Underwood)

81 Birthplace of Mrs Miniver

Position: Whitchurch is about 3 miles N of Aylesbury.
O.S. Map: Aylesbury area; Sheet 165; 1/50,000.
Map Ref: SP 804/204.
Access: The Priory, now the Priory Hotel and La Boiserie restaurant, is in the High Street.

Remember 'Mrs Miniver', that rose-coloured portrayal of the rural middle class made in 1942? Besides Greer Garson, it starred Walter Pidgeon, Richard Ney, Dame May Whitty, Teresa Wright and Helmut Dantine, and won seven Oscars. Its creator, Jan Struther, lived and grew up here in Whitchurch, the village from which she drew her inspiration for the film.

Jan Struther (real name, Joyce Anstruther) lived in the Tudor Priory – once a courthouse, now a hotel – which stands among other attractively built houses in the High Street. She wrote a number of hymns, which appear in *Songs of Praise*. She is buried in the churchyard ofthe nearby St John the Evangelist Church under her married name of Jan Plachzek.

Places of Interest in the Neighbourhood
When Hampden Said No (Aylesbury)
Unknown Warriors (Hardwick)
Queen Elizabeth I Dined Here (Quarrendon)

82 In Loving Memory . . .

There's nothing morbid about strolling around churchyards: at best, they can be interesting; at worst, places for quiet contemplation. Many graves are described in the main text of this book, but here are some others, with details about where to find them.

First, a local tragedy. In Wycombe Cemetery, Benjamin Road, *High Wycombe* (map ref: SU 868/938), there is a broken column grave containing victims of a serious accident that occurred at the turn of the century. During the digging out of the Whitehouse railway tunnel, Loudwater, near High Wycombe, in 1902, the tunnel roof collapsed, crushing six men to death and injuring another three. The only local

The grave of six railway navvies killed in 1902.

G. K. Chesterton's gravestone, sculpted by Eric Gill.

man was Harry Morton (23), who lived at Knaves Beech. This memorial, erected by public subscription, is in section E of the cemetery.

Novelist, racehorse owner and gambler Edgar Wallace (1875-1932), author of more than 170 novels and plays (including *The Four Just Men* and *Sanders of the River*), is buried in Fern Lane Cemetery, *Little Marlow* (map ref: SU 882/887). He lived at Bourne End, but died in America.

The scientist Sir William Ramsay is buried in the churchyard of Holy Trinity, Hazlemere, *High Wycombe* (map ref: SU 888/953). He discovered several chemical elements, and won the Nobel Prize for chemistry in 1904. There is a memorial window in the same church to D. Philip Barnes, founder of the Royal Botanic Society, who died in 1874.

In St Mary and All Saints Church, *Beaconsfield* (SU 946/900), there is a modest brass plate set in the floor of the seventh pew from the front on the south side of the nave, marking the burial place of the great

123

political theorist Edmund Burke (1729-1797). The poet Edmund Waller (1606-1687) has an imposing memorial in the churchyard.

There are tombs and memorials to members of the family that once owned *The Daily Telegraph*, including Edward, the 1st Baron Burnham (1833-1916), Viscount Burnham, who died in 1922, and Edward, the 4th Baron (died 1963).

The 1st Marquess of Lansdowne (1737-1805), who was briefly Prime Minister (1782-1783), is buried in the family vault in All Saints Church, *High Wycombe* (map ref: 865/934). Lord John Russell (1792-1878), Prime Minister 1846-1852, is buried in the family chapel at *Chenies* (map ref: TQ 015/985).

Critic, novelist and poet G. K. Chesterton (1874-1936), who lived in Beaconsfield for 26 years, is buried in *Beaconsfield Cemetery*, near the Shepherd's Lane entrance (map ref: SU 947/904). His headstone bears an interesting sculpture in relief by the artist, typographer and designer Eric Gill.

In *Chalfont St Giles* churchyard (map ref: SU 991/935) lies the circus owner Bertram Mills (1873-1938), who staged circuses at Olympia year after year from 1920. He lived locally at Pollards Wood.

A cleric who became a great Bible scholar, the Rev Thomas Scott (grandfather of the architect Sir George Gilbert Scott), lived at *Aston Sandford* (map ref: SP 756/078) (a hamlet near Haddenham), where he was rector. He died there in 1821, and is buried under the altar. Scott was a founder of the Church Missionary Society, and produced a famous Bible Commentary in weekly parts, which became a classic, earning him the sobriquet Scott the Commentator.

Finally, a man who, as his headstone says, 'devoted his life to the safety of aircrew': Sir James Martin (1893-1981), engineer and inventor of the aircraft ejection seat, which has saved thousands of lives. The company he founded, Martin Baker, is at Higher Denham. Sir James's grave is in *Old Denham* churchyard (map ref: SP 043/870).

Index

Places by page number

The Curiosities of England

The following titles in the series have already been published and can be ordered at all bookshops, or in case of difficulties direct from the publishers.